ASTRAL

Discover the Greatest Human Delusion of **ALL TIME**

BUSTING KARMA THROUGH THE INVISIBLE LANDSCAPE OF YOUR SOUL

PAMM MILLAGE

First published by Ultimate World Publishing 2024
Copyright © 2024 Pamm Millage

ISBN

Paperback: 978-1-923123-68-7
Ebook: 978-1-923123-69-4

Pamm Millage has asserted her rights under the Copyright, Designs and Patents Act 1988 to be identified as the author of this work. The information in this book is based on the author's experiences and opinions. The publisher specifically disclaims responsibility for any adverse consequences which may result from use of the information contained herein. Permission to use information has been sought by the author. Any breaches will be rectified in further editions of the book.

All rights reserved. No part of this publication may be reproduced, stored in or introduced into a retrieval system, or transmitted in any form, or by any means (electronic, mechanical, photocopying, recording or otherwise) without the prior written permission of the author. Any person who does any unauthorised act in relation to this publication may be liable to criminal prosecution and civil claims for damages. Enquiries should be made through the publisher.

Cover design: Ultimate World Publishing
Layout and typesetting: Ultimate World Publishing
Editor: Alex Floyd-Douglass

Ultimate World Publishing
Diamond Creek,
Victoria Australia 3089
www.writeabook.com.au

TESTIMONIALS

"I absolutely love hearing Pamm Millage present her divine teachings to the world. She is a true treasure trove of knowledge, and every time I listen to her, I feel like I'm receiving a gift of wisdom. Pamm has this incredible ability to align her teachings with a profound sense of connection and understanding. Her presentations are not just informative; they are transformative experiences that leave me feeling inspired and uplifted. Pamm's passion for sharing her wisdom shines through in every word she speaks, and I am incredibly grateful for the opportunity to learn from her. She is a true beacon of light in this world, and I am blessed to have her in my life."

- Patrisha Palmer, AHC

"Pamm, congratulations on writing ASTRAL! I feel so honoured to have edited your book and I must say, it's an incredibly special one. I really believe it's going to help a lot of people."

- Alex Floyd-Douglass, Editor

"Every now and then there is a book that will challenge you, and then reward you well for the effort. ASTRAL by Pamm Millage is such a book. How many books take you to the place where you discover who you are, what your purpose is and how you express the inner you? ASTRAL does this and a lot more. This excellent book took me on a journey and as with most journeys worth the effort there will be some challenges along the way. Some of your preconceptions may be re-thought after reading ASTRAL.

Having studied philosophy academically and as a life-long interest I can say this book adds greatly to the discourse. The Author says, 'Traditional psychology has not studied the evolutionary journey of soul consciousness beyond the observable.' ASTRAL attempts, successfully, to go past those boundaries into the realm of the unobserved.

In all the mental gymnastics here, the greatest skill of all is on the balance beam and what that means for you and the location of your purpose, and that is a journey well worth taking."

— Nigel Wilson, News Editor

"I am exceptionally blessed to know Pamm Millage, a living Master who has been pivotal in my personal and spiritual development and learning. Pamm is the embodiment of everything good that she teaches in her wonderful book ASTRAL.

ASTRAL demystifies the questions that bewilder most of us about the vast invisible world within and beyond our earthly experiences and comprehension. Mysteries of birth, life, death, and between lives are revealed alongside the integral part that humans play in the interconnectedness of all life. A very firm message is given that our vibrational frequencies impact on everything on this

TESTIMONIALS

planet with responsibility lying firmly on the individual to embrace that knowledge with awareness and action for the well-being and evolution of, not only the self, but also for our beloved planet. To this end, Pamm emphasises, the importance of daily spiritual practices, with examples given, to enhance our awareness and commitment to embodying the 'highest ideal consciousness possible.'

I loved this book and highly recommend it to anybody needing to make sense of life. Jam-packed full of infinite wisdom this book contains the keys to finding peace in our frequently disturbed world."

— **Kate O'Connor, Clinical Hypnotherapist and Acupuncturist**

"Having been looking for guidance on where to go from here, having travelled so far in my life journey already, I didn't know where to look but I knew I needed more. I had many titbits of truth, gleaned from research and life experience. In ASTRAL I have found what I was seeking. An overview, a framework, a concise gathering of the fundamentals as well as practical steps to help me move forward. ASTRAL has it all; our purpose, karma, ego, protection, chakras, affirmations, discernment, choice, dimensions and so much more. ASTRAL brought together aspects that I knew but it gave structure and meaning - as well as a path I can now follow that resonates with me so incredibly deeply.

'Knowing yourself is the beginning of all wisdom.' - **Aristotle**

For those seeking answers and understanding beyond what many can provide; in these pages you will find what you are looking for."

— **Sara Williams, Creator, Flowers & Faeries**

DEDICATIONS

To YOU who KNOW your space is ALL space.
And each one of us creates from our place.
NOW is the time to pick up the pace.
Now is the time to
FILL ALL SPACE WITH GRACE.

To YOU who aren't sure and are willing to know.
Your glory is waiting, you can give it a go.
Dis-ease and dread may fill your day.
The choices are here for
A BETTER WAY.

If how you were then, is how you are now,
The trouble may be that you don't know how,
To wake yourself up when the timing is right!
There is no darkness.
THERE IS ONLY LIGHT.

ASTRAL

If you're one of the ones who don't 'give-a- feck',
You'll carry on trucking and ignore that you're 'steck.'
You're one of millions; there are more than a few!
BLESSINGS ARE GIVEN TO THEM
AND YOU TOO.

To Carl and Gary, my beloved sons,
Thank you for you; you are the Ones!
I love you more than ever you'll know.
We have given each other
BIG SPACES TO GROW.

To Barry, my husband, a man of good stead,
You support me regardless of what flows from my head.
You stick by me and endow me with love,
FOR YOU I THANK THE GOOD LORD ABOVE.

- Pamm Millage

ACKNOWLEDGEMENTS

To those Great Masters who have gone before.
Your words are infused with a golden awe!
Enlightening my mind at silent times.
Frequently now with quirky rhymes!

The force of your words is an opening door.
The answers to questions put forward before.
By millions of souls looking for more,
Joyfully found in Divine Natural Law.

To the movers and shakers with passion they serve.
To the teachers, the coaches, the leaders with nerve.
To those who stand for the good of the ALL.
Too many to name from near and afar,
Thanks to you too; you know who you are.

ASTRAL

To patients and colleagues both then and now.
Teachers and students swap roles somehow.
Working through stuff to stand in our truth.
Healthy new lives are the true signs of proof.

To Julie and Vivi, Nat, and Stu.
This book wouldn't be if it wasn't for you.
Thank you for giving me space to show,
My readers new secrets and places to grow.

Alex Floyd-Douglass, I acknowledge you too
To edit my words was my mission for you.
Most readers don't know of the lengths that you go
To mentor and show an easier flow
for them to absorb new things to know.

CONTENTS

TESTIMONIALS	iii
DEDICATIONS	vii
ACKNOWLEDGEMENTS	ix
INTRODUCTION	1
CHAPTER ONE: WHO THE HECK ARE YOU?	11
CHAPTER TWO: 'Y' IS A CROOKED LETTER!	19
CHAPTER THREE: ANYONE FOR DOMINOES?	25
CHAPTER FOUR: DIRTY SHADES OF GREY	33
CHAPTER FIVE: THE THREE LITTLE PIGS	43
CHAPTER SIX: THE COMPANY YOU KEEP!	63
CHAPTER SEVEN: LOVE'S RESONANCE	73
CHAPTER EIGHT: 7 SACRED SECRETS	79
CHAPTER NINE: THY WILL BE DONE!	95
CHAPTER TEN: THE POINT OF EQUILIBRIUM	111
CHAPTER ELEVEN: ENERGETIC YOU	119
CHAPTER TWELVE: KEYS TO MASTERING YOUR EARTHLY PERSONALITY	133
CHAPTER THIRTEEN: FORT KNOX AND THE GOLDEN EGG	141
CHAPTER FOURTEEN: BUSTING THE KARMA DRAMA	151
CHAPTER FIFTEEN: PHYSICAL BRAINY STUFF!	177

CHAPTER SIXTEEN: SUPERPOWERS	191
CHAPTER SEVENTEEN: THE BALANCING ACT	203
CHAPTER EIGHTEEN: THE FICKLE FACES OF FEAR	213
CHAPTER NINETEEN: DIMENSIONS AND DENSITIES	225
CHAPTER TWENTY: BEST OUTCOMES	235
CHAPTER TWENTYONE: WHAT EVERYONE IS DYING TO KNOW	243
AFTERWORD	259
ABOUT THE AUTHOR	265
GLOSSARY OF TERMINOLOGY	269
BIBLIOGRAPHY	271
RECOMMENDED READING	273
HANDY LINKS	275

INTRODUCTION

TO THE SEEKER OF SECRETS

This book is written for you: the compassionate of heart, the seeker of peace, the seeker of wisdom, the seeker of joy, the seeker of love, the seeker of secrets, the seeker of answers to the mental mayhem that holds the health of the world to ransom.

> *"There is a greatness awaiting you!*
> *You may be busy; you may be distracted.*
> *You may be cynical.*
> *But this greatness is patient – it waits!*
> *This greatness finds you in a moment,*
> *unlikely or untimely.*
> *And suddenly you find yourself*
> *connected to ALL humanity.*
> *In a way that shocks you!*

ASTRAL

*And this greatness will hold you up so high and strong,
That any previous version of yourself seems flimsy."*
(Anon)

CHALLENGES, TREASURES, AND SECRETS

Herein lies the challenge!

Purging the delusion of fear allows the space for you to experience and maintain a life of joy.

The treasures and secrets you uncover as you read through to the end of this book will not only expand your personal consciousness, but also infuse you with new depths of wisdom, love, and personal power – the vital components to living a purposeful life.

Within the quirky but poignant paragraphs, you will find you recognise truths that at some level you already knew but had tucked away in the secret chambers of your mind.

ATTITUDE AND WELLBEING

The personal experiences I share are purely to more clearly elaborate on the point of truth that is being channelled to you, the avid evolver of your own fascinating journey on Earth – and beyond!

My encouragement is to enlighten your attitude, to allow more informed choices, to take right action; and to use your enormous creative power to regenerate your own wellbeing. Hence, to reclaim the exquisite gifts of your birth right.

INTRODUCTION

TRUTHS AND SUBTLE ENERGIES

This book unleashes truths that have been lost,
to most of the global population for far too long.
Across all our systems we are in more than a bind,
Symptoms perhaps of the blind leading the blind?

There are subtle energies beyond your own thinking that can both negatively and positively influence your life. When you know what they are and learn how to harness their power, you will recover your own magnificence. You will realise the real purpose of your existence and you will be hoodwinked no more!

"Mind is the Master-power that moulds and makes,
And Man is Mind, and evermore he takes,
The Tool of Thought, and shaping what he wills,
Brings forth a thousand joys, a thousand ills:
He thinks in secret, and it comes to pass,
Environment is but his looking glass."
(James Allen)

ONENESS AND PURPOSE IN A CHAOTIC WORLD

Across the ages, at any time of crises – such as the events of today's world – there has been a spiritual awakening that allows humanity to take the next evolutionary step. Although many of us are active within the current awakening, the questions are:

Why haven't we done this yet as a world population?

Why is there so much chaos within the environment which is our looking glass?

THE ROLE OF AWARENESS

There are those that rebel and those who step forward.
It is those who raise awareness who must be applauded!

It takes courage, determination, and enlightened thought to gather and integrate the psychology of spirit, science, motivation, and knowledge necessary to act rightly and wisely in any situation.

THE UNITY OF DIVERSITY

Whether you're a son; a father; a sister; a brother;
a daughter; a mother, or something other!
We are all the same as one another.
Whoever you are and whatever you do,
You are the only one that can empower (or disempower) you.

IT IS NEVER TOO LATE TO CHANGE YOUR FATE

No matter what your role is in life,
Accepting yourself totally will save you from strife.
To make healthy and lasting systemic change
both personal and global – across the whole range.

As the ancient Greek philosopher Heraclitus said,
"The hidden harmony is better than the obvious."

Heraclitus meant that deeper truths, hidden beneath the surface, hold greater value and significance than what is immediately apparent. By finding the harmony within yourself and others, you can help create a more peaceful and prosperous world.

INTRODUCTION

THE WISDOM OF THE AGES – THERE IS NOTHING NEW

So many masters have gone before and shared their ageless wisdom in volumes of Sacred Law and beautifully inspired words. Alas, at times, fruitlessly.

In the ALL that is ALL, all ideas exist.
But there are some ideas that you may have missed.
Through the eons you've lived your many lives through.

What is your purpose? Who are you?
How do you express your unique view?

IS THE TIMING RIGHT FOR YOU?

Timing is crucial for understanding wisdom, as Hermes Trismegistus said,

"Words of Wisdom fall only on the ears of understanding."

Hopefully, now is the right time for you, dear reader, to grasp the purpose behind these words. This book aims to convey timeless wisdom in modern language, fostering a reactivation and integration of mind, heart, body, and spirit.

I invite you to temporarily set aside your subjective truths as we embark on an exploratory journey into your mental alchemy.

When you have read this manuscript all the way through,
You can make powerful choices that are right for you!

1. Your 'subjective truth' is shaped by your current perceptions, beliefs, and past experiences.
2. Exploring your 'Invisible Beingness,' the energies within and around you, may lead you closer to understanding your evolutionary journey towards the 'Absolute Truth'.

HUMAN GOLDFISH

The cycle of life it comes, and it goes
Repetitive patterns in ebbs and flows
Like goldfish swimming around the bowl;
Whatever is missing from making us whole?

The same things we do day in and day out
The same things we get on life's roundabout.
How do we reach our evolutionary goal?
The only way out is to work with the soul.

To spiral awareness to the highest mind
Through the soul, to the Spirit of Truth you will find.
You've always known; let's open the gate!
ALL gifts are yours to use and create.

Assuming you are a compassionate individual seeking deeper insights into your Being, it's recognised that each person's perspective is unique. Sacred Principles and Natural Laws affecting universal health and harmony are conveyed in diverse ways to resonate with your truth. In this era of change, it's crucial for caring individuals to act with integrity in the current cycle of karmic evolution.

Regardless of our individual humility, those with merciful and harmless intentions must strive to co-create positive change within

INTRODUCTION

all systems on the planet, both material and natural. This begins with harmoniously integrating your own inner and outer energy systems, then extending this integration to your spheres of influence: family, friends, colleagues, and passions. Every individual contributes to the whole, inspiring powerful awakenings within themselves and providing spaces for others to make informed, healthy choices.

Throughout history, humanity has been unconsciously indoctrinated with skewed beliefs, leading to a worldview clouded by fear, anger, and powerlessness. This has fuelled barbaric behaviours such as violence, greed, and corruption, all stemming from a sense of lack, fear, and personal powerlessness.

Within these pages:

1. You will discover practical solutions to things that may have held you back in expressing the best of yourself.
2. You will deeply consider why you as an individual are on the Earth at this time in its history.
3. You will have the opportunity to make some powerful choices for your own harmony and overall health.
4. You will understand how you so powerfully effect the harmony of planetary and cosmic events.
5. At the very least you will have an expanded awareness of the invisible world of your life and creation.
6. Once you have digested this material you will never be the same as you were when you started reading – you will have evolved your consciousness!

ASTRAL takes you on a journey into those invisible realms that influence every individual's wellbeing. At times, we will look beyond to the impact you as one person have on the collective unconsciousness of today's world and vice versa: both negative and positive. Perhaps there is more to global warming, conspiracy theories, reckless behaviours, pandemics, greed, wars, corruption, and pandemonium than meets the common eye?

My words come from a heart filled with love.
Channelled with wisdom from Heaven above.
My deep concern for our beautiful Earth
Is my purpose for living, my reason for birth.

It appears to me that authoring this book was predestined; just as anyone's unique purpose is. What I have learned through many personal challenges and in ignoring many inspired ideas, is that <u>you cannot get away with anything if it is not on track to your own higher purpose</u> and reason for living in this demanding Earth school.

THE LAW OF KARMA

The Law of Karma will make sure of it. You are a being of many dimensions that are 'screaming' to be harmonised to fulfill your destiny. No one else can do it for you. You are an instrument in the great orchestra of LIFE. Your instrument is unique, and no-one can master its tune but you.

We all make mistakes, and I have made my share!
Acknowledging mistakes can lay you bare
To the impact you have on those out there.
You can't live your life on a wing and a prayer.

What you receive and you see everywhere
Reflects your innermost thoughts to give you the dare
To find gifts in all challenges which serve to enhance
The awareness and clarity for you to advance

INTRODUCTION

Your health, your power, your wisdom, and love
Through your soul to the virtues of your spirit above.

As you bring your best virtues back to earth
You will find your own purpose for this life's re-birth.
No matter what it is that you constantly do
No one can do it; no, only you!

I acknowledge that this book conveys similar messages in various styles, intended to enrich your understanding. When you align your conscious and unconscious mind, greater transcendence occurs within you. The aim here is not to instil guilt or fear but to inspire forgiveness, compassion, and a joyful existence marked by heightened consciousness.

By highlighting disparities among groups and individuals, the goal is to offer enlightenment and encourage genuine transformation. Those living with good intent are not to blame for being influenced by the egoic mass consciousness. Similarly, individuals unaware of the power of their own unconscious are not at fault.

As you become aware of these aspects, it becomes your responsibility to either accept or take command of them.

This, ultimately, is the purpose of living on Earth.

Disclaimer: The information provided in this book is for educational purposes only. The exercises suggested in this publication are not intended as medical advice. To comply with current medical ethics, it is advised that individuals with medical conditions or concerns seek guidance from a healthcare professional before attempting any of the exercises mentioned. The author and publisher disclaim any responsibility for actions taken based on the recommendations in this book, whether used by the reader or others.

CHAPTER ONE

WHO THE HECK ARE YOU?

"God is man minus ego."
(Shirdi Sai Baba)

Does that mean YOU ARE GOD when Ego is conquered?

Before we get under way
I just want to say...
This book is inadequate!
For it cannot relay
How much more magnificent you are,
than these words can portray!

ALL LIFE IS GOD-CONSCIOUSNESS DIFFERING IN DENSITY AND DIMENSION

THE MATERIAL ISSUE

Many people prioritise physical appearance and material wealth, often to extreme lengths, as portrayed in cosmetic surgery TV shows, for example. However, basing your identity solely on external factors blinds you to the profound power of your inner and outer spiritual world. Awareness of both positive and negative invisible energies can greatly impact life on Earth, influencing progress and karma.

THE GOLDEN KEY TO THRIVE

To achieve a healthy and joyful life is to prioritise the positive influence of your Spirit over earthly matters. Your soul acts as a bridge between your earthly self and your Divine Spirit, expressing your highest consciousness. Thriving on the path to self-realisation and connection with the Divine requires transcending the negative ego's duality and integrating life's polarities.

Your soul is pure consciousness; the core of which is LIFE.
Distortions in your consciousness can create a life of strife.
Life, the fire of spirit, breathes the desires of your mind.
Your situation, body, and environment, you will find,
Tell you when you're up to play or falling far behind.
You resonate and vibrate to creations of your thought.

Are you happy? What's happening in your world?
Are you healthy? Are you peaceful?
Or are you overwrought?

OUR EARTHLY SCHOOL

You have a body and so do I
You live on this Earth; do you wonder why?

WHO THE HECK ARE YOU?

*The Earth is a hard but temporary school
Until you know what you need to know to grow
Your wisdom, your love, your power to create.
If you don't do it now, you'll reincarnate.*

But you get millions of chances to graduate!

*You know what I mean, you've done it before
Time and again, you've missed opening the door
To break the chains of karmic law.*

THE NEGATIVE EGO

*For aeons of time, you have been a sponge
Unconsciously hypnotised by too much grunge
The subjective beliefs of devil-may-care
Millions of people so unaware.
Dispensing negative ego everywhere.*

*There are many dimensions that make up you.
'Though the body you have is temporary too
It's useful for taking the actions required
To realise your goals and the ideas you've inspired.*

*It's urgently time to de-hypnotise
And clear the smut from your physical eyes.
For what you see may not be true*
Unless it echoes the Divine in you!

Humanity's negative ego arises from pessimistic thinking rooted in distorted beliefs about superiority, attack, judgment, self-worth, anger, power dynamics, and bully-victim mentality. This spectrum ranges from minor jealousies to outright malicious intentions and destructive actions, reflecting varied levels of manipulation and behaviours.

<u>Evil</u>, the extreme form of negative ego, wields significant influence in society, causing suffering and devastation. Acknowledging its presence is crucial for taking proactive measures against it. Awareness and understanding are essential for navigating life responsibly and joyfully.

AGELESS WISDOM – SPIRITUALISING MATTER

In the Ageless Wisdom teachings any action towards improvement is defined as 'spiritual.' Humanity's journey on Earth is to learn how to spiritualise matter. This generally refers to the idea of imbuing or elevating physical or material aspects of existence with spiritual significance or qualities. It implies a perspective that sees a deeper, transcendent meaning or connection within the physical realm.

In spiritual or philosophical systems, the material world is seen as a manifestation of a higher spiritual reality and the process of spiritualising matter involves recognising and attuning yourself to this underlying spiritual essence. It involves cultivating a heightened awareness, or a sense of sacredness in everyday activities and physical surroundings.

Spiritualising matter can also be associated with the transformation of your perception of material possessions or physical experiences. It may involve transcending mere materialistic or superficial concerns and finding deeper meaning, purpose, or connection within the physical aspects of life; in a harmonious manner for living healthily on Earth.

Ultimately, the interpretation of 'spiritualising matter' can vary depending on the cultural, religious, or philosophical context in which it is used. Each belief system remains 'subjective' until individuals embark on the personal journey of clearing the pathway to 'Absolute Truth'.

Regrettably, a substantial portion of the global population grapples with the challenge of discerning where to initiate this profound exploration.

THERE IS NOTHING NEW

The methods and ideas contained within this volume are based on ageless wisdom, natural laws, Hermetic principles, esoteric psychology, and the teachings of the ascended masters who have gone before. There is nothing new.

<u>ALL exists in the ALL of the Great Eternal Mind that is YOU and ME</u>.

Bit by bit over centuries of time, small seeds are re-sown in the minds of humans; and decade after decade more humans take up the call that echoes within. The call to return home to the divine mind of our eternal essence.

Although concepts relating to consciousness, metaphysics, and the exploration of the mind are fascinating and have intrigued humans for centuries, it does not help humanity that most of them do not fall within the current scientific paradigm.

Metaphysics, in particular, delves into questions beyond the scope of traditional scientific inquiry, exploring topics such as the nature of reality, consciousness, and the interconnectedness of existence which is the topic of this book. However, while these ideas may not always align with current scientific understanding, they can contribute to broader conversations about the nature of human experience.

HEAVEN IS WITHIN YOUR STATE OR MIND!

To truly make a difference and live a joyful, authentic, and loving life, you must consciously confront aspects often ignored. It's easier to stick with the familiar, but exploring one's inner and outer mind is essential for growth.

Throughout history, miraculous healings have been dismissed as quackery, and those who dared to be different faced persecution. Great achievements arise from imaginative ideas and the courageous pursuit of higher ideals.

While dreaming is important, it's the integration of willpower and action that manifests creation, reflecting the Sacred Hermetic Principle of Gender.

CONSCIOUSNESS IS ETERNAL

Consciousness is a centre of <u>pure awareness</u> with nothing in it but potential, until the Creator in you forms it with the living light of thought — ideas, images, emotions, and commands, such as the Almighty perfect, and joyful Creation of you, completely egoless in its original blueprint.

In your ideal, you are connected by pure Living Light to ALL that exists in the Omniverse. Of course, there are other sacred cosmic ingredients too...

WHO THE HECK ARE YOU?

COLOURFUL AND BEAUTIFUL YOU!

You have a <u>personality ego</u> which differentiates you from your brothers and sisters in this world. It is the unique expression of who you are – radiating your SPARK OF LIFE, your compassion, your authenticity, your learnings and yearnings, your love, your wisdom, your joy, your power, your right actions, your willingness, and all the highest virtues you acquire as you grow. Colourful and beautiful you!

It has a name – 'The Edenic State', or your perfect human and spiritual blueprint which you gradually move back to in the process of ascending your awareness and taking right action.

Yes, we can all make mistakes, however, if your intentions are harmlessness, compassion, and kindness; you may forgive yourself and others and move on – <u>there is no bad karma</u>.

But what is in the way of your experiencing this?

CHAPTER TWO

'Y' IS A CROOKED LETTER!

Odd things happened on the way to today.
Mysterious forces got in the way.
Where did they come from?
Where do they Go?
In the heights of your mind
You'll find,
You already know!

KNOCK, KNOCK, KNOCK!

At times it's a tapping, at times it's a knock,
This time is different, it's a knock and a rock!
Tap-tap-tap; knock-knock-knock.
My body is rocking to the beat of the clock.
Persistently knocking, persistently rocking!

"Somebody behind me is playing silly buggers!" I think. I'll ignore them.

It is 2021; the second day of conference and I'm in brain fog. It's early afternoon and I haven't presented my paper yet. I have the last slot of the day.

I'm feeling grumpy. My mind is wandering back to my less-than-ideal studio bed and breakfast perched on the edge of one of New Zealand's idyllic tourist attractions. Lake Rotorua is surrounded by a thermal wonderland of experiences that I have no time to enjoy on this visit.

When booking my accommodation, the online pictures sold me on the beautiful view and returned my memory to the adventures of childhood vacations. What a let-down! The experience is somewhat different. The weather is muggy, there is no air conditioning, and I can very nearly touch the ceiling with the palm of my hand which is quite a feat for someone so 'short'.

Two days later, I am not rejuvenated after the five-hour drive to the venue. What's more, I feel completely discombobulated by an inexplicable explosion of noise from the loudspeaker I am sitting beside. I've always had a 'thing' about noise. As a child, I was told I had 'ears like a bat' and not in the literal sense. It was useful for hearing conversations through the wall but not so great in a cacophony of sound.

I'm imagining tomorrow when I can put the top down on my new red convertible and head further north to visit my older sister. It's been a long time since I saw her. Another two hours driving each way will be worth it...

Whispers in my ear bring my mind back into the conference room; the prodding continues. Rather annoying really. I abruptly turn around to catch the 'silly bugger' behind me. It is highly unusual for me to be out of my 'space of grace' and to be feeling on edge.

"Oh! My!" I say to myself. "There are other invisible energies at play here."

All eyes and ears of the audience behind me are dutifully focused on the big screen which hangs from the ceiling three rows in front.

I turn back towards the front, out of my reverie now. I am vaguely aware of the continuous tapping on my shoulder as the keynote speaker looms on the screen. His presentation is streaming from across the world. He looks very authoritative, and he has the entire audience's attention. He is marketing his new protocol; inviting those hypnotherapists present to sign up to learn it for themselves.

Suddenly, a stark realisation hits me – I can't align with his words. The whispers in my ears have vanished, and the presenter's voice now resonates crystal clear. I'm alert, and the prodding sensation ceases.

"I don't know where our thoughts go," he utters, *"But..."*

The prodding resumes, accompanied by louder whispers insisting that this issue must be addressed. This man, a renowned teacher and therapist with influence over many minds, openly admits uncertainty about the destination of thoughts. Surprisingly, this is something I assumed my hypnotherapy colleagues would have grasped during their studies, especially before working with emotional clients. Did he perhaps miss that crucial day?

WHAT DOES ASSUME DO?
IT MAKES AN <u>ASS</u> OUT OF U AND <u>ME</u>

I know the saying is not new to you
But I had to remind myself again too!

He is now taking questions from the floor. Reluctantly, I overcome the urge to stay seated and risk humiliating him. Invisible forces propel me to my feet, my legs feeling like jelly. Taking a deep breath to centre myself, I address him with respect.

"With great respect," I hear myself say. "Do you protect yourself and your clients energetically when using this protocol?"

The immediate response is evident in his body language – arms folded across his gut, a defensive question mark hanging in the invisible ethers above his head, and eyes shooting virtual darts my way. I've caught him off guard, achieving precisely what I sought to avoid – humiliation.

"What you resist, persists," I silently reproach myself. Internally, I apologise, yet deep down, I sense that this entire incident was meant to unfold. The question lingers: Why?

'Y' IS A CROOKED LETTER AND 'Z' IS NO BETTER!

'She was a curious child was Pamm', they say,
She asked 'Why?' at least 10 times a day.
Driving us crazy with all her 'Whys?'
To know how things work; and 'Why no replies?'

The frustration worked both ways of course.
To Pamm 'no answers' were an added remorse.
'Y' is a Crooked Letter and 'Z' is no Better!
Answers like this made Pamm a 'fretter'.

In the times before TV, websites, and Google,
Information was scarce and answers were frugal.
When the day finally came to go to School
She was scared but elated and felt super cool.

'Y' IS A CROOKED LETTER!

She learned how to read with Janet and John.
Soon fairytales were what she focused upon.
When the encyclopedia salesman came to the door
With Arthur Mee's knowledge she lay on the floor
And buried her head in new text to explore.

The 'Whys?' they continue to this very day.
Stupid answers to questions are just not OK!
A response from a teacher one day 'off the wing'-
was 'Too much information is a dangerous thing!'

'But why? Tell me why'.
There was no reply.

It wasn't long before she made up her mind,
That in Nature were answers she was looking to find.
The Natural and Invisible Laws she explores,
Bring enlightenment and wisdom that infuse her pores.

Researching the workings of the human mind
And the why are we here? And the how do we find?
True peace and harmony and Heaven on Earth
It's all here and now, the inheritance of Birth.

In the higher dimensions of your Magnificent Mind
All health, all wealth, all answers you'll find.
Compassion; forgiveness, justice, and Love
The ideals and virtues of Goodness Above.

"Until we make the unconscious conscious,
it will direct our lives and we will call it 'fate."
(Carl Jung)

CHAPTER THREE

ANYONE FOR DOMINOES?

YOUR LIFE PURPOSE AND
THE LAW OF CAUSE AND EFFECT

"Sometimes things have to happen before other things can happen!"
(A Boy Called Sailboat, Cameron Nugent, 2018)

TRIGGER #111 - THE CAUSE

Back to the conference. Stunned at my own behaviour, I plonk myself down in the chair in disbelief; and begin to quietly beat myself up. Louder whispers now – I hear clearly in my mind, *"Sometimes things have to happen before other things can happen,"* and immediately a quiet peace washes over me. All I must do is trust in the process.

FOR EVERY CAUSE, THERE IS AN EFFECT
AND FOR EVERY EFFECT THERE IS A CAUSE

Nothing happens by chance. The Sixth Hermetic Principal of Cause and Effect which in turn relates to the Law of Karma is in the pot stewing. This law states that every action produces a corresponding reaction. It highlights the concept of karma and encourages you to take responsibility for your choices and their consequences; for you reap what you sow! The Law of Cause and Effect is held in the 4th dimension of consciousness where you use the power of your thought and mind to create your own version of reality.

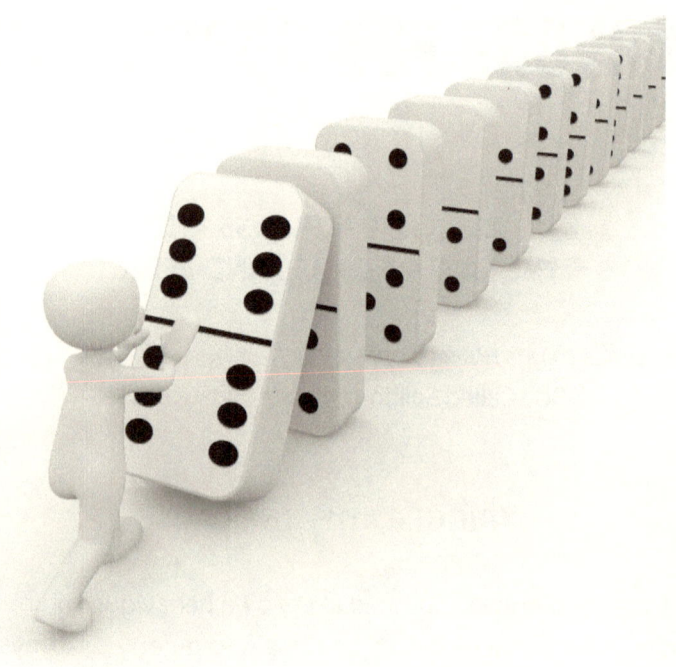

*"Every cause has its effect; every effect has its cause.
Everything happens according to natural laws.
Chance is but a name for Law not recognised.
There are many planes of causation,
but Nothing Escapes the Law."*
(The Kybalion)

THE EXPONENTIAL EFFECT OF ALL CAUSES AND EFFECTS IS TO FIND THE GIFT THAT COMES WITH EVERY CHALLENGE

Like dominoes every effect provides a cause for other effects. To be the cause of all your effects requires you to be mindful of all your thoughts, emotions, and actions.

My self-critiquing continues; and I begin to understand what further action is required on my part. The Divine Whispers recur consistently. I listen to them for two years until the full significance of <u>the gift that comes with this challenge</u> emerges.

The 'Ah-ha!' compounds and clarifies the effect of other 'signs' I have ignored for decades as I have continued to grow my knowledge. I must now act wisely to fulfil my reason for being on Earth at this time of its evolution. This humble being is required to share what I have learned and know to be true. Right NOW, IN THESE PAGES is the time for enlightenment my beloved reader, on where thoughts and emotions go and what they do when they get there!

BUT FIRST, HUMANITY'S GENERAL LIFE PURPOSE

The general purpose of life on Earth is to individually self-actualise in an enlightened and integrated way to end the cycle of karmic reincarnation. Impersonal Love, Wisdom, and Personal Power are the ingredients to transmute your state of consciousness to an expression of your ideal or 'God-self.'

Your Consciousness is Sacred and Eternal whether or not you are breathing or physically alive. It is when you are aware of it and take command of it that makes the difference.

ASTRAL

ADHERING TO YOUR LIFE PURPOSE HELPS DISSOLVE YOUR KARMA

Adhering to your life purpose aids in dissolving your karma. Your journey on Earth involves evolving and synthesising spiritual energies, beliefs, and actions back to the Divine Essence. By recognising and acting upon the gifts within challenges, you can evolve your consciousness and transmute destructive energies. Fulfilling your unique purpose is essential, as it impacts not only your inner energy system but also your environment and beyond. Each person's contribution to the greater Oneness is significant in shaping harmonious existence.

KNOWLEDGE AND RESPONSIBILITY

I return to explore, what I sought to explore before:

'Too much information is a dangerous thing?'
'But why? Tell my why?'
There was no reply.

Now I see why there was no reply.
<u>Not enough</u> knowledge
Is the real reason why.

Grow your awareness
From what you already know.
When you know what you don't know,
You'll know some more.

Open your mind; open the door;
Explore and explore and explore galore,

ANYONE FOR DOMINOES?

*Then you'll know that you know,
that you don't know more!*

However, with knowledge comes power and responsibility:

"The possession of Knowledge, unless accompanied by a manifestation and expression in action, is like the hoarding of precious metals, a vain and foolish thing. Knowledge, like wealth, is intended for use. The Law of Use is Universal, and he who violates it suffers by reason of his conflict with natural forces."
(Hermes Trismegistus)

ROADSIGNS TO YOUR UNIQUE LIFE PURPOSE

The correlation between becoming unconsciously competent and having a unique life purpose is grounded in the journey of personal growth, self-awareness, and meaningful contribution (service). As you gain proficiency and mastery in areas that resonate with your passions, it may very well serve as a road sign or a significant clue pointing toward your unique life purpose.

*Evolving your goodness makes your heart sing.
The spiralling dynamics is an eternal thing.
Discovering your joy in what you love to do,
Will show you your purpose is unique to you.*

Let's explore how being <u>unconsciously competent and passionate</u> can be related to finding your own life purpose:

1. **Alignment with Natural Talents and Interests**: Unconscious competence arises from a blend of natural talents, acquired skills, and genuine interest. Your life purpose may align with

areas where you are passionate and proficient. Exploring your various talents and how they correlate can unveil your uniqueness.
2. **Flow State and Fulfillment**: Unconscious competence often leads to a state of flow, where engagement in an activity brings deep fulfillment and joy. Experiencing flow indicates alignment with your life purpose.
3. **Unique Contribution (Service):** Unconscious competence in a skill or domain can empower you to make a significant impact and create meaningful change. Leveraging your expertise serves your life purpose of contributing to others or society.
4. **Inner Calling and Intuition**: Passion and unconscious competence are intertwined with inner guidance toward your life purpose.
5. **Sustainable Motivation**: Being unconsciously competent in areas aligned with your life purpose provides intrinsic motivation to persevere through challenges. Mastery amplifies the impact of your contributions, driving positive change in your world.

While being unconsciously competent in something you are passionate about can be a valuable road sign, finding your life purpose is often a multifaceted and evolving journey. It may involve exploring different areas of interest, reflecting on personal values and virtues, seeking guidance from mentors or advisors who can help you elicit your values and staying open to new experiences and opportunities. Personal growth and self-discovery play significant roles in uncovering your life purpose, and the intersection of passion and unconscious competence can be a powerful guide along this transformative path.

ANYONE FOR DOMINOES?

Your skills and your passions, they want to come out.
You can dodge and shove and go round about.
But there's no way round, you must follow through,
With the Ideas and insights that come to you.

Living your own purpose is what you're here for
Or you'll be back to Earth to repeat what you've done before.

THE LIVING LIGHT OF LOVE AND GRATITUDE

When you begin to recognise the 'gifts in every challenge' you go through, while collecting the skills, wisdom, and passion to live your life purpose, you may then experience the gratitude you feel to know why you undergo the dramas and traumas. It really does hone the diamond that you become to know the WHY and take right action with grace and gratitude.

At times, you may need to 'fake it until you make it' in your practice. However, if you are consistent, you will always know that you can prove the laws within this book. You can make them real and embody the virtues that hold you in joy and enlightenment no matter what your purpose is.

My Note to the Cause of Trigger #111 (The Presenter)

I am so grateful to you who gave me the impetus to act. The domino effect is exponential. If you ever read this and recognise yourself, I hope you understand your important part in the co-creation of this book.

Somewhere on the invisible landscape of our souls in another dimension between birth and rebirth, we made a contract. In this instance, you provided the Cause, and I provided the Effect for more causes and effects.

You helped me stand in my power; and perhaps I helped you develop your wisdom further – only you will know the rebound effect I caused for you.

I send you blessings always...

BEING WILLING TO FORGIVE SELF AND OTHERS IS THE BIGGEST KEY TO HEALING AND SPIRITUAL FREEDOM

The fascinating point here is that we are all teachers and students of each other. That is what relationship is about. Relationships all give opportunity to grow. The quicker you can raise yourself above drama and respond in a win-win way, the quicker you will know and accept yourself and others without harsh judgements.

Forgiveness of self and others is one of the most critical areas to conquer. Having a willingness to forgive and practice <u>involved detachment</u> will take away the inner chaos. At the core of my Being is a knowing that you and I are here for a higher purpose. The purpose that ignites the flame within and gives you the opportunities to live a joyous, healthy, and powerful life.

Yes, there is a greatness awaiting you!

> *"He who is devoid of the power to forgive is devoid of the power to love."*
> (Martin Luther King Jr)

CHAPTER FOUR

DIRTY SHADES OF GREY

RISING ABOVE THE EGO'S DIRTY SHADES OF GREY

In comparison to your unique and beautiful gifts, the <u>negative ego</u> is that which expresses all the dirty shades of grey that exist within the many different layers of fear-based emotions. Fear comes in many guises. It is what sullies the beauty of the true essence of who you are. Fear-based traits are man-made lowly, negative egoic emotions and re-actions created by similar process to love-based traits, but with much lesser ingredients.

In Divine Absolute Truth, most fear is an illusion or a misperception that is not as it appears. <u>The gift in every challenge</u> is in rediscovering that. However, it drives people to behave atrociously at times and do shocking and disastrous things.

Although we all suffer from the same syndrome
Our Spirit heeds the call to come home.
Producing for us dramas ideal
to transcend the ego and help us heal.

Relationships with self and others too,
Give insights into who really is you.
How we see our world gives us all the chance,
To divide and conquer or
Harmonise and Enhance.

This time round is a good place to start
To fulfil your purpose through the grace in your heart.

IDENTIFYING YOUR EARTHLY EGO

The duality of your human ego refers to your sense of self which can exhibit both positive and negative aspects. It embodies a spectrum of qualities that range from selfishness, pride, and attachment – to compassion, self-awareness, and growth. This duality recognises that ego can have both constructive and detrimental influences on your thoughts, behaviours, health, and relationships; highlighting the importance of self-reflection and personal development to navigate and transcend its negative aspects.

At the core of all psychological work there are only two emotions, love, and fear in all its guises. A conceptual understanding of how to identify and release negative ego is vital in the process of evolving yourself. All of us have lifetimes of experience, experiment, study, and practice – consciously, unconsciously, and super consciously; traumatic, and joyful within the invisible dimensions of energy and power that is formed by mind and imagination within 'The Law of Mental Alchemy.'

The Law of Mental Alchemy is the Hermetic principle that suggests by changing your thoughts and beliefs, you can transform your reality and experiences. It asserts that your mind has the power to shape your life, and by cultivating positive thoughts and actions whilst focusing on desired outcomes, you can manifest changes in your circumstances. In essence, it highlights the connection between your thoughts and the material world you create for yourself.

Albert Einstein said, *"The world we have made as a result of the level of thinking we have done thus far, creates problems that cannot be solved at the same level we created them."*

THE SCHOOL OF HARD KNOCKS

The School of Hard Knocks embodies life's challenging experiences governed by the Law of Karma, including the profound struggles of 'the dark night of the soul.' These hardships aren't imposed by a divine will but are opportunities for self-confrontation and growth. Suffering serves as a catalyst for releasing entrenched patterns and seeking a more fulfilling path.

The extremes of this are symbolised by Christ's 40-day and 40-night ordeal in the desert, often referred to as 'the dark night of the soul' reflecting a universal process of inner transformation when individuals are lost in deep despair.

*At which stage the only way out is up – or not!
Each is free to choose their lot.*

Despite the ideal vision of learning through grace, most souls navigate life's lessons through the demanding curriculum of the School of Hard Knocks. As individuals collectively undergo these lessons, global chaos emerges, shaped by collective experiences. Embracing transformative power and adopting approaches shared in this book can guide towards spiritual integration and resilience, contributing to a more enlightened world.

THE CHRIST PRINCIPLE

1. The metaphorical life of Jesus Christ serves as an example for humanity, illustrating principles of love, compassion, forgiveness, and selflessness, guiding individuals towards living harmoniously with one another and with the divine.

2. The principle of the 'Christed Heart' transcends time and the historical figure of Jesus Christ, representing a state of divine consciousness and unconditional love that exists within each individual. It signifies the awakening and embodiment of Christ consciousness, wherein you align with the highest spiritual truths and express love, compassion, and unity in all aspects of life.

DIFFERENTIATING SOUL AND SPIRIT

There exists a common confusion regarding the distinctions between the soul, the Spirit, and psychic abilities. It is essential to recognise that these facets are not synonymous.

<u>The soul</u> represents the innate consciousness of life, lacking the higher realisation of preceding and forthcoming worlds. It undergoes numerous formations, transformations, and rebirths before intertwining with divine consciousness.

Understanding that the soul differs from the Spirit allows you to seek and pray for elevated knowledge and wisdom. This pursuit leads to the bestowal of the 'Holy Spirit' of higher reason, granting inspiration and comprehension of the intricate levels and workings of the eternal Divine Mind. The evolution of consciousness is perpetual, offering extraordinary adventures once the negative ego is transcended.

<u>The Spirit</u> signifies the reunion of the soul with the harmonic cognisance of the 'I AM THAT I AM' identity with the Godhead, the Source of all love, light, and creative energy in the vastness of the ALL that is. Spiritually realised beings embody this presence on Earth in the undertaking of their divine life purpose in service to the Divine Plan.

THE MERGING OF TRADITIONAL PSYCHOLOGY AND SOUL PSYCHOLOGY – I WISH!

It is recognised that the distinction between these approaches is not universally accepted, and the terminology can vary across different philosophical, spiritual, or psychological traditions. Some practitioners integrate spiritual or soulful perspectives into their psychological work, while others prefer a strictly empirical and scientific approach.

To experience the mental, emotional, physical, and spiritual health necessary to live this earthly life in joy, there are three levels to ground and integrate within your heart, your consciousness, and your actions:

1. Physical/earthly living.
2. The psychology of mind and emotions.
3. The psychology of the Spirit which is attained through the evolutionary journey of soul consciousness.

Although the terms 'traditional psychology' and 'soul psychology' are not universally defined or agreed upon within the current field of psychology, and interpretations may vary among individuals or within specific subjective belief systems, the general understanding is:

TRADITIONAL PSYCHOLOGY

- **Focus:** Traditional psychology typically focuses on the study of the mind and behaviour, often from a scientific objective and verifiable perspective.
- **Approach**: It tends to investigate and understand mental processes, emotions, and behaviours through <u>observable and measurable</u> means. Traditional psychology often employs methods such as experiments, surveys, and clinical observations.
- **Scope:** The emphasis is on understanding the individual's conscious and subconscious mind within the context of the observable and measurable aspects of human behaviour.

Traditionally psychology has not studied the evolutionary journey of soul consciousness beyond the observable.

SOUL OR SPIRITUAL PSYCHOLOGY

- **Focus**: The term 'soul' or 'spiritual psychology' is an approach that goes beyond the traditional boundaries of psychology and incorporates elements related to the soul or spiritual aspects of human existence.
- **Approach**: Soul psychology involves <u>exploring concepts</u> such as the superconscious mind, spiritual growth, and higher states of consciousness. It draws from spiritual and philosophical traditions such as the ageless wisdom of esoteric psychology, Hermetic principles, and <u>the legacy of past spiritual masters</u>.
- **Scope:** This approach considers aspects of human experience that extend beyond the immediate, observable behaviour and delve into deeper invisible dimensions of consciousness, including the soul or spiritual essence.

DIFFERENTIATING LIGHTWORKERS AND PSYCHICS

LIGHTWORKERS

In essence, we are all Lightworkers, resonating as Beings of Light with varying degrees of vibration. Our physical bodies, the densest Light Bodies, anchor us to Earth, facilitating our life purpose and karmic resolution on the journey back to Divinity. Overcoming obstacles is essential in this pursuit.

Historically, those identifying as lightworkers embody compassion and noble intentions for the planet. However, while many possess advanced spiritual knowledge, they may overlook the unrefined psychological aspects of earthly living, necessitating integration for holistic health and self-realisation. Synthesising earthly living with both the psychology of the mind and the psychology of the soul is often neglected in education.

Good intentions may be tainted by past conditioning, mass consciousness, and misinformation, leading to corruption and manipulation by those with malicious intent. This can result in lightworkers and empathetic individuals falling victim to powerlessness, evident in conflicts and mental health issues. Recognising this and drawing inspiration from ascended Masters who overcame similar challenges, offers hope for lightworkers seeking to heal the world.

Although some younger generations have demonstrated an integrated approach to their Lightwork, it remains a minority. This book aims to expand wisdom, promote love, and encourage individuals to be consistent in their power to manifest good intentions through wise actions.

ASTRAL

PSYCHICS

Psychic abilities initially function on a subconscious level, distinct from the superconscious gifts that emerge as you integrate your spirit into everyday life. Many individuals are captivated by psychic powers without realising that they can pose significant pitfalls and traps on the spiritual path. Some individuals exhibiting clairvoyance, clairaudience, claircognisance or clairsentience may inadvertently channel negative astral entities or malevolent beings from within the nonphysical dimension of the astral plane of negative emotions.

Although the psychic's abilities transcend the conventional five physical senses, their possession does not necessarily signify spiritual growth or the quality of their channellings. The essential lesson and cornerstone of the entire spiritual path lies in the development and integration of earthly living with the higher polarities of consciousness. Without this harmonious balance, the psychic frequently learns the necessity for psychological protection the hard way.

There are many well-known psychics who assist police in helping solve crime; and who assist grieving people in coming to peace with the passing of their loved ones. And that is commendable. These psychics often demonstrate an amazing ability to contact the dead, and often see or experience traumatic events unfolding in the course of their work.

However, the risks some take and the mental and physical trials they go through can be debilitating until they integrate the energies necessary to discover and work with the divine energies that can keep them safe. Many have been through this arduous journey, and many have not.

DIRTY SHADES OF GREY

A psychic with a loving heart and good intentions is commendable. However, any messages that carry negative or fear-based connotations reveal the naivety of an untrained spiritual mind, potentially fostering a fear-based 'expectation' that contributes to its manifestation. This awareness is particularly pertinent for the secular, non-spiritually trained mind. You will understand why as you read on.

Where your thoughts go, your energy flows!

CHAPTER FIVE

THE THREE LITTLE PIGS

There are Three Schools of Spiritual Evolution on Earth:

1. **The Hall of Ignorance**
   Identification with the material world and the physical being.
2. **The Hall of Learning**
   Restlessness and a search for the knowledge of the self or soul.
3. **The Hall of Wisdom**
   Realisation, expansion of consciousness, and Identification with the spiritual self.

Congratulations!
Just by seeking more knowledge of yourself and your soul
You are now enrolled in both the Hall of Learning
And the Hall of Wisdom, however...

YOU CAN'T TAKE YOUR HEAVEN BY STORM!

Mastering and integrating your entire energy system is the key that defines consciousness development. Thought therapy or attitudinal healing is to work on yourself in terms of raising your thoughts and emotions on all levels: conscious, unconscious, superconscious. And to take the right action accordingly.

First, there are some things to be clear about. If you want to live in harmony and discover and maintain your inherent state of perfect wellbeing, you cannot take Heaven by storm! Your physical body would not survive it; nor would you mentally and emotionally be able to handle it. There are steps to take along the way that only you can take and be responsible for. The foundations have to be laid first.

LAYING THE FOUNDATIONS

When building your earthly home, you start from the first (ground) floor. If you started from the second or third floor, your house would have nothing to stand on. The steps to building the inner resilience necessary for you to embody and experience the magnificence of your innate birthright are threefold.

1. <u>Self-actualise the Personality</u>   (Linear timeline: EARTH time)
2. Self-actualise the Soul   (Vertical multi-dimensional: NOW time)
3. Self-actualise at a Monadic Level   (Eternal <u>Omnipresence</u>: NO time)

Take the analogy of the Three Little Pigs. When you build a house on strong foundations like the third little pig's brick house; this represents the foundation for your <u>Self-Actualised Personality</u>.

When the foundations are shaky as in the straw or stick houses; the heavy dark energies of stress, fear, anger, self-doubt, chaotic emotions, bad behaviours, and traumatic events, mean the Big Bad Wolf (the inner and outer negative egoic manifestations of your world) can quite subtly at times, come along, cause havoc, and blow your house down!

YOUR FOUR EARTHLY EGOIC BODIES

The four bodies of earthly egoic or duality personality are formed by the energy that feeds their potential.

FOUR - The Mental Body (invisible): Holds the thoughts and imaginings that influence the emotional or astral body.

THREE - The Emotional or Astral Body (invisible): Holds the emotions held in the physical brain and influences the etheric or health body. Love stems from the heart and is the eternal spiritual connection and communicator of health, whereas fear-based emotions do the contrary.

TWO - The Etheric Body or Health Body (invisible to most): The Etheric body is the blueprint that is influenced by the mental and emotional body. The fluctuating energy (depending on your mental and emotional states) within this invisible blueprint permeates and influences the physical body.

ONE - The Physical Body (visible): The physical body Is the body of action and reaction that is greatly influenced by emotion; both negative and positive (ease or dis-ease).

ASTRAL

YOUR FOUR BASIC PHYSICAL HEALTH BODIES

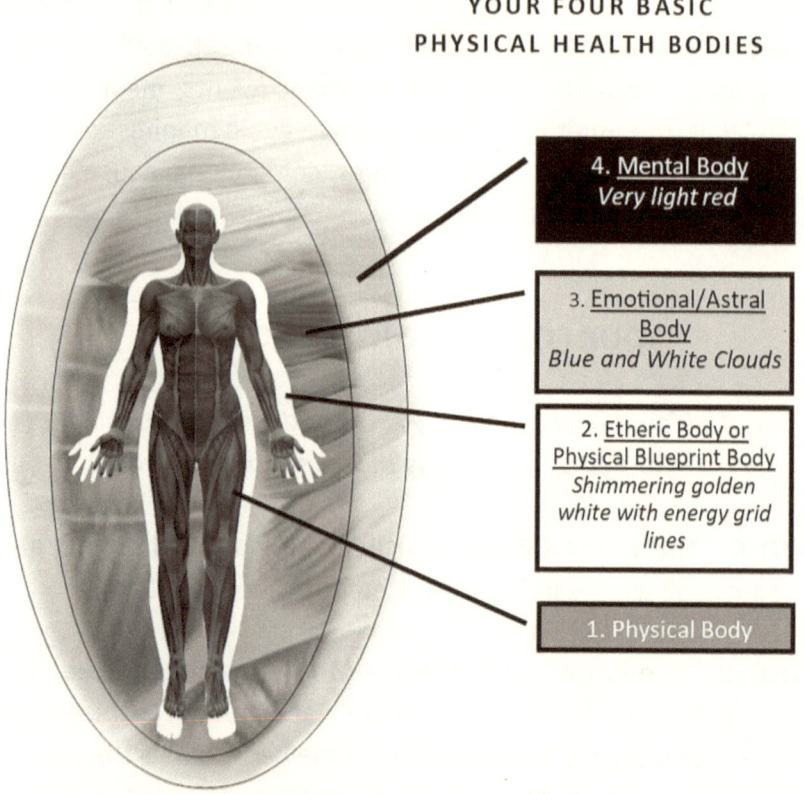

4. Mental Body
Very light red

3. Emotional/Astral Body
Blue and White Clouds

2. Etheric Body or Physical Blueprint Body
Shimmering golden white with energy grid lines

1. Physical Body

In metaphysics and spiritual circles, the 'etheric blueprint', 'health body' and 'aura' are frequently interconnected in describing the fluctuating states of your energy and emotional well-being. Trained practitioners, such as energy healers or aura readers, can see or interpret the colours and shades within these fields to gain insights into your emotions and spiritual state.

Kirlian photography is a known other means of capturing the colours and shades within your etheric body; although there is 'scientific' discussion that these images may be influenced by moisture and chemicals within the photographic process.

LIGHT BODIES AND COLOUR RAYS

As you continue your journey towards spirit actualisation, you'll become increasingly aware of the various invisible and colourful light bodies within your energy system. These bodies and colours hold incredible influences on your human experience. However, it's important to note that while they exist, I will not delve into them within this book, as they are beyond its scope and purpose.

AN <u>ENLIGHTENING</u> TOUCH OF SCIENCE **
(Ref: Biophotons in appendix)

- Light serves as a foundational element within the Human Being, with the human body functioning as a living photoreceptor.
- Consumption of light occurs through various processes, including the intake of light-infused food and photosynthesis.
- Remarkably, the nervous system and even DNA generate light, while each body cell emits over 100,000 light photon impulses per second, known as biophotons. These biophotons play a pivotal role in sustaining optimal health.
- The emission of light from cells facilitates information and energy exchange, crucial for effective communication between adjacent cells and steering the intricate web of biochemical reactions.
- Thoughts and emotions are composed of light in diverse densities and colours, contributing to the intricate tapestry of human experience.
- Breathing love and gratitude through the heart 'illuminates' neural pathways to the brain, enhancing the processing of added information and fostering overall well-being.

ASTRAL

- Recognising that all bodies are light bodies, with the physical body having the densest frequency, underscores the profound interplay between light and existence.
- Evolution of soul consciousness involves elevating the vibration of thoughts and emotions. This progression constructs numerous spiritual light bodies characterised by higher frequencies, vibrant colours, and influences beyond the four egoic bodies illustrated above.

YOU ARE A LIVING LIGHT BEING

Light is the main source of energy information and frequency
Light is the basic nutrient for ALL life.
<u>*It is the negative Ego that dims the light of LIFE*</u>.

ONE: THE PHYSICAL BODY

- Base structure of light or vehicle which encases the Light of God within and from which all other Light bodies are constructed.
- Constructed and created by God, the source of ALL, and the Elohim Masters.
- Consists of DNA, RNA, electrons, neurons, atoms, cells, blood, tissue, intellect, and consciousness.
- Your Divine Blueprint as an individual.
- <u>Influenced by the etheric body</u>.

TWO: THE ETHERIC/HEALTH BODY

- Protects and holds the blueprint or grid work for the physical body.
- One level of vibration up from matter.
- Golden/white shimmering appearance with the grid lines for the physical body flowing through it.
- This grid work is the foundation for electrical and Divine energy, impulse transmission, and reception for the physical Body.
- Transducer station for creative light emanation.
- A veritable <u>Geometry of Divinity</u>!
- <u>Influenced by the astral/emotional body</u>.

THREE: THE EMOTIONAL/ASTRAL BODY

- The emotional vehicle of an individual.
- It holds and manifests all emotional attributes.
- Thought forms created by your mind emanate through the emotional body.
- The emotional/astral body reacts and responds willy-nilly in the way consciousness dictates.
- Emotions influence the etheric/health body in clouds of varying degrees of density.
- As mentioned, emotional responses can be seen in the aura and chakra system, by the trained eye.
- **The emotional/astral body's vibration not only influences the etheric/health body and subsequently the physical body, but also takes your emotional frequencies to the corresponding dimensions of the astral plane where all emotional forms exist.**
- <u>Influenced by the mental body</u>.

EMOTIONAL/ASTRAL CAUTION

While lacking 'scientific evidence', the wisdom of those who have mastered their mind and energy systems, and shared their experiences, caution against the <u>lower astral realm of dark composition</u> – a place to be avoided whilst on the evolutionary journey of the soul. I am familiar with the subject matter, although I choose not to evoke my specific experiences in this instance. I am elucidating purely to let you know the hidden dangers of negative emotions and what to do to transcend them.

Emotionally vulnerable and desperate individuals including those who dabble in the dark arts or seek guidance from the inauthentic, frequently expose themselves to exploitation. Some enlightened spiritual therapists work with the releasement of souls trapped in the lower astral plane and at times, exorcise entities that attach themselves to the unaware. Navigating this dimension is not a fun zone to work in as a spiritual therapist but is possible with the assistance and protection of the 'God-Force.'

THE MENTAL BODY

- Expands into infinitude.
- The latitude of space the mental body has in which to work provides infinite possibilities.
- Holds all thoughts one thinks and <u>influences the astral body.</u>
- Holds the highest vibratory rate in the lower base structure of egoic Light bodies.
- You can control your thought creating ability.
- You can control and master your particular Spiritual essence known as your 'God-Self 'within every level of your Light

Bodies. You just have to integrate the work you do along the way.
- The mental body appears in the aura as red or ruby of the lightest hue.
- The mental body's vibration takes your thoughts, transmits them through all other Light bodies and into the universal mental plane where they circulate and influence.

'GOD' - A GROUNDING ACRONYM

In today's world, discussing God is not always commonplace. However, two earthly acronyms for GOD serve as grounded mental triggers for personal evolution and self-maintenance. These acronyms encapsulate powerful concepts, reminding of the divine essence within and encouraging us to transcend worldly distractions.

GOD - <u>G</u>eometry <u>o</u>f <u>D</u>ivinity
GOD - <u>G</u>race <u>O</u>ver <u>D</u>rama

THE LAW OF VIBRATION AND AFFIRMATIONS: A DIY 'PRACTICE RUN!'

Affirmation statements are powerful tools for fostering positivity. They serve as an effective do-it-yourself strategy when you have identified a belief or pattern that requires transformation, particularly if you have been harbouring negative thoughts or responding unfavourably.

In the upcoming chapters, you will discover the significance of daily positive affirmations. It is recommended to repeat these affirmations to yourself consistently, ideally multiple times a day, for a period ranging from 21-28 days for each negative belief you aim to transmute. This timeframe aligns with the duration needed to alter a habit. However, there are ways to expedite success.

Utilising affirmations proves especially beneficial when undergoing counselling, psychotherapy, or hypnotherapy. Essentially a form of <u>self-hypnosis</u>, affirmations are most effective when focused on one topic at a time. This approach allows for the rewiring of neural pathways, establishing a new positive pattern that aligns with your more authentic self.

HOW CAN SELF-HYPNOSIS HELP?

Most life experiences, around 90%, are shaped by the intricate patterns residing in your <u>unconscious mind</u>, a realm devoid of logical reasoning. The inherently illogical unconscious mind acts as a magnet, drawing or generating manifestations in accordance with its programming – primarily influenced by your personal encounters and, intriguingly, by unseen forces. Hypnotherapists specialise in guiding individuals to access their unconscious minds, facilitating positive transformations in deeply ingrained beliefs.

While your unconscious mind operates subtly beneath conscious awareness, steering and sometimes distorting behaviours and emotions through stored memories, the <u>conscious mind</u>, or intellect, engages in logical thinking, decision-making, and self-awareness. <u>Actively directing your conscious mind becomes crucial to realign the unconscious mind with your desired life outcomes</u>.

This conscious guidance serves as a means to synchronise both aspects of the mind. However, the journey towards authenticity and joy expands further when incorporating the <u>superconscious</u>

<u>mind</u> which with practice can <u>access divine inspiration</u>, unveiling a more genuine expression of self.

The future is yours; it already exists.
Step into the mould that fits and assists,
Sense it and feel it without delay.
For your future is now, there is no other way.

FIVE MAGIC KEYS FOR SUCCESSFUL AFFIRMATIONS
Remember to be compassionate to self
and harmless to ALL.

POSITIVE – PRETEND – ANCHOR
ACTIVATE – REPEAT

PPAAR

1. **POSITIVE**
Affirmations must be POSITIVE and stated 'AS IF' they are true right now.

Find a quiet spot where you won't be disturbed for this 3-5-minute internal imagery (self-hypnosis) practice exercise. You will find examples of affirmations beneath these keys to help you out. Practice makes perfect!
   (a) Take a small drink of water before you begin. Water takes the energy around your body. Find a comfortable position with feet on the floor.
   (b) Your conscious mind must accept and know your affirmation can be accomplished. If not, change the wording to suit what you consciously and positively want. Commit it to memory and close your eyes.

(c) Take three or four long full breaths in through your nose and out through your mouth. Full breathing is like mana from Heaven. It has been shown to reduce symptoms of anxiety by promoting a state of relaxation.
(d) Imagine yourself sitting in a violet vortex of light – see it burning off any fear or negative judgements.
(e) When you are ready change your imagery to surround yourself in a swirling golden egg of God's light of protection.
(f) Your conscious mind can now direct and retrain your unconscious mind.
- Water – comfort – feet on floor
- Memorise
- Eyes closed - Breath
- Violet Vortex
- Golden Egg

2. PRETEND

Fake it until you make it – ACT AS IF! Your unconscious mind won't know the difference.

(a) Engage your unconscious mind actively by evoking as many of your senses as you can – envisioning, sensing, feeling, knowing, tasting, hearing, seeing, smelling, and immersing yourself in the quiet joy of embodying your affirmation as if you are living it right now.
(b) Repeat the affirmation aloud and enhance the inner experience with elements like colour, light, love, gratitude, sound, and imaginings such as people congratulating you – whatever is essential for elevating your inner heightened emotional frequency. This magnetic force draws in both attraction and support as it communicates your desires effectively to your unconscious mind which is in constant creation.

(c) By elevating your passion and emotions to align with your desired outcome, you actualise your ideal polarity, counteracting the inner negativity.
- Engage your unconscious mind.
- Repeat aloud and enhance inner experience.
- Elevate and feel the positive vibrational change.

3. **ANCHOR AND SEAL**
Making it Real (REALISATION) is the rapid road to all change.

(a) Inhale your ideal vibration infused with love and gratitude. Bring it to ground within your body (embody) by placing your hand on your heart, forming a fist, or adopting a comfortable gesture of your choice. Some individuals find placing the tip of their tongue on the roof of the mouth behind their front teeth effective. Use whatever works for you.

(b) This anchor serves as a trigger, enabling you to revisit that heightened state of vibration during your affirmation practice. Simply employ the same body part (trigger) and engage your imagination to re-activate the elation. Practice.
- Inhale and anchor.
- Practice trigger.

4. **ACTIVATE**
Physical action reinforces and (ACTIVATES) it into earthly living.

(a) Take at least one action each time you affirm in order to reinforce your intent as if you are living it. Practice makes perfect!

(b) Be creative – *"Every day in every way I AM happier and healthier."* The first action could be to make a list of activities that support your health and happiness.

Happiness is a subjective experience, so it is different for everyone.

(c) Physical action — dancing a jig on the spot for a couple of minutes; taking a walk in nature; mowing the lawns; signing up for a course or massage; washing the car; having a shower... Consciously taking any physical healthy action with your new affirmation in mind employs more invisible forces of support.

Positive affirmations with heightened inner sensations + physical action = the activation of the Law of Positive Attraction

5. **REPEAT – REPEAT – REPEAT**
   (a) Write your affirmation on post it notes and stick them in places you see constantly during the day – e.g., mirrors, doors, fridge, phone...
   (b) Repeat your affirmation as often as possible. Practice makes perfect.
   (c) Use your trigger and breathing to assist.
   (d) Take actions that put your inner affirmation into motion on earth.

EXAMPLES OF AFFIRMATIONS MY CLIENTS HAVE USED

Note 1: You can use the examples below as a basis to create a psychological/spiritual affirmation that fits you perfectly. It must be a positive 'AS IF' statement.

Note 2: Although these examples are more general and subjective, when you have a tangible goal for your material life, the more specific you can get about what you want and how you feel when you get it follows the same process.

1. Every day in every way I AM happier and healthier
2. LOVE is my compass in Life.
3. I embrace and act upon the divine gift in every challenge.
4. I attract supportive and loving people into my life.
5. I practice harmlessness in all my activities.
6. Every day in every way I AM an authentic expression of my divine self.
7. I wholeheartedly express my divine wisdom, love, and power.
8. I AM capable, resilient, and worthy of the amazing transformation that is under way.
9. Every day, in every way, I AM fitter and healthier.
10. I AM perfect whole and complete.
11. I AM worthy of receiving all that is good.
12. I integrate all my divine energies in a harmonious, AUTHENTIC, and supportive way.

BEDTIME AFFIRMATIONS:
A 'SUPER-FUEL' FOR FASTER RESULTS AND BETTER SLEEP

Last thing before sleep and first thing when awakening when you are still in your sleepy relaxed state is an ideal time to use your affirmation. This sleepy state is akin to the somnambulistic state hypnotists sometimes use to help you rewire your unconscious thoughts and beliefs to positive outcomes.

1. Keep hydrated during the day – water takes energy around your body.
2. Ideally you will have had a physically active day and eaten light and nourishing food several hours before bed. NB: Coffee and alcohol before bed is an inhibitor to both sleep and this exercise.

3. At the end of your day, complete your daily bardo – see below.

Word of Caution: This technique is inhibited if your phone or television is on in the bedroom at night. The blue/white light from digital products disrupts the natural production of melatonin, which facilitates your circadian sleep rhythms.

Sleep time pointers:

- Lie down and get cosy.
- Violet Vortex.
- Whirling Golden Egg.
- Affirm once and release.
- Focus on your long full breathing.
- Surrender to sleep.

THE DAILY BARDO

The 'Daily Bardo' serves as a daily audit of your experiences, preventing the accumulation of unresolved psychological issues and fostering growth by extracting insights from spiritual tests and lessons. Committing to this practice facilitates self-realisation and deepens your connection with your divine being.

Keeping a journal to record progress and inspirations is highly beneficial as it allows for reflection and can yield valuable insights over time. Much of the wisdom in this book has originated from reflections found in personal writings over decades.

Many people write a list of things they have on their minds or need to attend to tomorrow before they leave work or go about their evening tasks. Similarly, if you wake with something on your mind, you can jot it down for retrieval the next day.

MORNING AFFIRMATIONS: A 'SUPER-FUEL' FOR A GOOD DAY

PPAAR
Positive; Pretend; Anchor; Activate and Repeat

On waking while you are still sleepy in bed repeat the five magic affirmation steps. Remember to breathe and weave the golden egg of God's protection. This will set you up for the day.

HEAVENLY HEALTH

When you regularly add genuine feelings of gratitude and love to your breathing, imagining it as golden platinum light infusing into your heart, lungs, and solar plexus you can soon bring your body back into its natural state of homeostasis (self-healing) for longer and longer periods. Happy! Happy! Joy! Joy!

When you know what you don't want in your life, you have the key to finding the opposite which is <u>what you do want</u>. if you can manage the practice above and follow the exercises within these pages, you will be empowering your soul's evolutionary journey through this book with an open heart – well on the road to experiencing more deeply your authentic self.

THE ABSOLUTE TRUTH

In ultimate reality (Absolute Truth vs subjective truth) your true essence is already aligned with the ideal. However, human experiences can entangle the mind in fear reactions and distorted negative ego 'baggage,' giving rise to unconscious false beliefs and patterns. These patterns function as barriers to your authentic divine self.

During certain life challenges, you might have overlooked the inherent gifts within them (a common experience for everyone). As you gain awareness of these missed opportunities, you embark on the journey of retraining your unconscious mind through affirmations, and other transformative methods.

Evolving your consciousness
Means becoming aware.
of the 'IS'NESS of ALL...
of Everything, Everywhere!
And then knowing it too

Way beyond just me and you!
Eternal ONENESS, the I AM that I AM
The power, the love, the wisdom all through
The essence of life, that INCLUDES YOU.

DIY

While it's entirely feasible to embark on a 'Do it Yourself' approach, enlisting the assistance of a registered professional hypnotherapist can significantly expedite the time required for the process. Although it is not necessary, it can be more profound to enlist

THE THREE LITTLE PIGS

a professional hypnotherapist with spiritual training; one who collaborates with the super-consciousness mind to access Divine intervention for more integrated results.

Of course, we will be discussing this in more depth... BUT HEAR THIS!

<u>YOUR UNCONSCIOUS MIND IS YOUR BEST FRIEND IF YOU KNOW HOW TO HANDLE IT WELL!</u>

CHAPTER SIX

THE COMPANY YOU KEEP!

Regarding your life's journey and your reason for living on Earth, Yogananda said that, "The single most important aspect is the company you keep."

Let me clarify that this chapter aims to make a general observation rather than cast accusations. Yogananda's insight holds true as a massive portion of the global population finds themselves inadvertently ensnared as powerless victims, absorbing the unseen thoughts, behaviours, and emotional energies of those around them.

The unconscious mind functions like an absorbent sponge, soaking up a continuous stream of information, whether it be visual, auditory, contemplative, judgmental, or ingestive; throughout the day and night.

While your brain employs an unconscious filtering mechanism based on instilled higher values and virtues, the methods and rationale for assuming individual responsibility in attitudinal healing have often been overlooked by generations past.

Why?

The passage of time has allowed for the transmission of skewed information and, at times, unscrupulous manipulation for self-serving purposes.

The worldwide manifestation of mental, emotional, spiritual, and physical ailments represents just one facet of a population that seems far from awakened and responsible. Managing your own emotional baggage is undoubtedly a substantial task, and the added concern of external influences only amplifies the challenge. Thus, navigating the complexities of personal healing becomes an even more pressing endeavour.

PEOPLE COME INTO YOUR LIFE FOR A REASON, A SEASON, OR A LIFETIME

It takes determination, willingness, and grit to carefully choose the company you keep and to safeguard your personal power regardless of external circumstances. The most vital relationship is the one you have with yourself. Inner peace enables you to serve others simply by being.

The subtle, negative energies of others can impact you if you are unaware and unprotected. Every experience has a purpose, and challenges serve as gifts to help you realise your ideal self. The key is to identify and embrace these gifts, acting authentically with harmlessness and respect toward yourself and others.

We are all both teachers and students.

Judging others often reflects unaddressed aspects within ourselves, leading to recurring scenarios until we acknowledge and transform them with love and gratitude. This process may involve forgiveness, acceptance, reclaiming personal power, or practicing detached compassion.

In life's journey, not all relationships are meant to be everlasting. Some serve a specific purpose or offer valuable lessons for a time (a reason), others are transient (a season), and some endure for a lifetime. Recognising the transient nature of relationships allows you to evolve, reclaim self-love, embrace self-responsibility, and develop self-knowledge. The layers of personal growth are vast, requiring practice to change ingrained reactions. For instance, uncovering the purity of spirit demands an ongoing effort to shift entrenched responses. Here is one of my personal examples:

A REASON

*I get off the bus
And stop in my tracks
Something's amiss
But I don't know the facts.*

*I feel uneasy in my heart and my gut
I adjust my stance and walk fast in a strut.
300 meters I'll be home and dry!
Next thing I know, there's a pain in my thigh.*

*It's a small pellet from a BB gun.
'Bugger the pain', I start to run.
Two boys on the road; one is my pal
Have taken to tormenting this College gal.*

*They use my butt as a target to shoot
They make their first hit and let out a hoot!*

ASTRAL

'A smoke for a poke!' They shout at me
As with all my might I try to flee.

My mind is confused
I don't understand.
I'm trying to escape
this swamp of quicksand.

'I don't know what you mean,' I say
'And I don't smoke anyway!'
'Come to the Cove, we'll show you now.
We've got a surprise! We'll show you how.'

Although I don't know what's happening to me
My heart and my gut tells me to flee.
My adrenal glands are in full flow
Giving me strength to 'up and Go!'

I arrive home and fall through the door
And recall vague memories from long before
Times when I had no voice or choice.
This time I realise the gift and rejoice.

I reclaim my power, as I sit on the floor
This time, I choose to be victim no more!
Thanks for the lesson I think today.
(One of many I have to say!)

VIBRATIONAL OSMOSIS WITHIN THE COMPANY YOU KEEP

Osmosis: In simple terms, osmosis is when a substance (usually water) crosses a semipermeable membrane in order to balance the concentrations of another substance. This happens spontaneously and without any energy on the part of a cell.

Vibrational osmosis as it affects you is a process by which values, meanings, emotions, and beliefs are learned and lived and transferred back and forth between and among persons; in essence having a conscious, and unconscious effect. Being aware of this now, will help you think more deeply about the company you keep and the thoughts you think, which will give you the power to make more life enhancing choices.

I personally use a variety of this method to retain my research. As an avid researcher, I frequently sleep with books under my pillow, especially when my intellect needs to understand something written in a convoluted way. In which case, I hold the intention of absorbing the messages more clearly. My books in this instance are the 'company I keep' along with the God-force I commune with. It never ceases to amaze me, when I am cogitating on an issue, that the very book I have under my pillow will open its pages on the exact solution I am looking for.

THE GOD-FORCE

Recognising the absence of negativity within the goodness and purity of God is essential, yet awareness alone is not sufficient. The dynamic relationship between Humanity, Shamballa, and the Hierarchy constitutes a complex interplay of spiritual forces and consciousness. Shamballa represents the apex of humanity's spiritual attainment, embodying the divine Will of God's intentions. The Hierarchy acts as a bridge between Shamballa and humanity, embodying qualities of Love and guiding spiritual evolution.

The concept of the 'God-Force' is a collective of beings with exceptional skills and healing abilities, each expressing a unique aspect of the divine. Seeking assistance from the God-Force aids in integrating and harmonising your energy system and enhancing the efficacy of personal affirmations.

While on this journey of discovery, initiating contact with spiritual forces necessitates caution and discernment. Calling upon Archangel Michael for assistance with God's Golden Egg of Protection before invoking the God-Force safeguards against potential interference from astral realms. The ultimate objective is to establish a direct and conscious relationship between Humanity, Shamballa, and the Hierarchy.

The transformative teachings of Alice Bailey underscore the importance of operating from a soul-centred perspective in this conscious relationship. Invocation of spiritual forces accelerates spiritual progress, stimulates soul expression, and catalyses positive global transformation. This evolutionary process entails aligning with higher values, understanding the Christ Principle, and fostering a heightened resonance in collective consciousness.

THE HUNDREDTH MONKEY EFFECT ON THE UNAWARE

'The Hundredth Monkey Effect' (Lifetide, Lyall Watson, pp. 147-148. Bantam Books 1980) is a demonstration of where I am headed in explaining the invisible realms of consciousness, the company you keep and the interconnectivity of the ALL.

The Hundredth Monkey Effect is a term that is said to have originated from an observation of Japanese macaques on the island of Kōjima. One macaque discovered a new way of washing potatoes. The story suggests that when a certain critical number of monkeys (the 100th monkey) learned this new behaviour, the same behaviour of washing potatoes spontaneously spread to other monkeys on nearby islands without any direct communication. This story is often used to illustrate the idea of a collective critical mass consciousness, or tipping point such as the vibrational osmosis discussed above.

It is important to remember that the hundredth monkey effect can work both ways; for good and for not-so-good. Take the mass psychosis of conspiracy theories, social media influences, bullying, sub-cultures, and societal group behaviours. Other great influences can be the media, films and even the news you watch. This illustrates the necessity for psychological protection on your invisible journey to self and God realisation.

ECHO CHAMBERS AND THE MEDIA

I consider echo-chambers to be a similar process to vibrational osmosis. A scenario could be the sharing of conspiracy theories on social media which stimulates many expressions of anger, hatred, and blame. It is not long before those who listen or participate become angry and ugly themselves.

Why?

Because the messages echo and re-echo within the chambers of the mind; both consciously and unconsciously. As with an affirmation, or new idea, the patterns of the mind can be changed, at times with reverse effect when you are unaware and unprotected.

Considering the influence we all have on the company we keep; it becomes evident that all systems possess the potential for both advantageous and disadvantageous impacts on the general public. Society strategically leverages various avenues to exploit the media, an influential force that reaches the majority of the population, thereby granting it considerable power to shape public perception, from fostering negative expectations to driving advertising agendas.

Individuals often grapple with a myriad of negative expectations across diverse topics, be it global news, violent movies, war reports, or media projections of world events like 'global warming.' In the face of manipulations involving fear, anger, revenge, and judgments, it remains crucial to stay informed by listening to reports while maintaining a detached emotional involvement – a mindful strategy aimed at preserving mental and emotional harmony.

VIBRATIONAL OSMOSIS WORKS ON MULTIPLE LEVELS

Vibrational osmosis can work on multiple levels of density which means it can affect the biology of the unaware either negatively or positively. *'The Biology of Belief'* written by microbiologist, Dr Bruce Lipton, presents his own experiments on epigenetics, exploring how your cells receive and process information. In short, among his scientific conclusions are that energy messages emanating from your positively vibrating or negatively vibrating thoughts can have a profound effect on your wellbeing. Modern transpersonal hypnotherapists working within higher consciousness practice energy healing methods every day to assist in more profound healing for their clients.

Metaphysicians, such as the late Louise Hay, may well have been delighted for the scientific back up of what she had proven for herself by her own cancer healing experience. Louise Hay's book, *'Heal Your Body'* was my 'Bible' when I first started out in professional hypnotherapy. It not only explores the emotional stress or <u>dis</u>-ease behind diseases of the body, but also gives beautiful affirmations to rewire your unconscious thoughts, helping you to align with what you consciously want.

There are many similar volumes since written and I have listed some in the appendix for your reference. Before moving on, I also want to mention *'The Power of Love & Gratitude'* by Dr Darren R Weissman, and *'The Hidden Messages in Water'* written by the late Dr Masuru Emoto, who, before he transitioned to his next spiritual adventure, gave me permission to use images of his experiments on water.

Both Weissman and Emoto illustrate how higher vibrating divine thoughts have a healing effect on the molecular structure of both blood and water respectively. This in turn has an effect on physical cells and DNA, dependent upon the quality of vibration maintained.

YOUR PHYSICAL BODY IS YOUR TEMPORARY EARTH VEHICLE

Your physical body is your temporary vehicle on earth to self-actualise and learn the lessons of LIFE which will eventually lead to the synthesis of all the blissful gifts of your birthright. Note, I said 'eventually'. It is a process that takes dedication and time but will break the shackles of karmic reincarnation.

It will set your Spirit free.

But first, you must heal your inner unconscious negative attitudes and beliefs and have them align with what you want consciously and super consciously, beyond which resides the ideal dimension of your 'Monad' or 'God-self''.

KARMA AND REINCARNATION

Karma is the principle that every action carries consequences. The energy you project into the world will eventually return to you, whether in this life or the next. It's a simple equation – if your words and actions are positive, good things will come your way; if they are harmful, you can expect unfavourable outcomes.

The added twist as suggested is that Karma isn't confined to just your actions; it extends to your thoughts and intentions. So, negative thoughts or intentions like jealousy and revenge also generate energy that circles back, offering you an opportunity to discover the lesson in each challenge.

We'll explore the intricacies of karma and personal power in more depth in the upcoming pages.

In the interim, a mere willingness to embrace harmlessness, forgiveness, and love can guide you through the journey.

CHAPTER SEVEN

LOVE'S RESONANCE

PLANET EARTH RESONATES WITH THE EMOTIONS AND ACTIONS OF ITS POPULATION

'EARTH' AND 'HEART'
Same Letters = Same Vibration

What is within your heart?

Are you practicing harmlessness, forgiveness and compassion for self and others?

IMPERSONAL LOVE:

SYNCHRONISING OUR HEARTS WITH EACH OTHER AND THE EARTH

As you utilise various methods such as love-based breathing and living light meditations to elevate your spirit and support mental and physical health, your heart will begin to sing.

Blessing what you eat and drink with gratitude is a practice rooted in the understanding of water's consciousness. The waterways of the world reflect the importance of our current way of being and the impact of thoughts and emotions on the world around us.

By sending love without attachment, we can assist in the transcendence of challenging situations for ourselves and others.

BLESSINGS

Feeding drama with worry makes it worse
The negative energy becomes a curse.
When love and blessings fill the space
Drama dissolves in glorious grace.

Awareness gives the power to discern
And the love you send dissolves concern.
Surrendering to your higher powers
Rains miracles in colourful showers.

When you realise how creative you are
You will understand that you're a Star!
Creating good in your Living Light
Helps unchain us all from a desperate plight.

NEUROPLASTICITY AND THE GOLDEN SEA OF LOVE

Remaining mindful of these practices and visualising God's swirling golden sea of love and gratitude as a protective energy egg in daily life not only fosters beautiful vibrations and security in the heart and gut regions, but also illuminates numerous neural pathways in the brain, supporting neuroplasticity.

Neuroplasticity is your physical brain's ability to change and adapt throughout life. It involves the formation of new neural connections, the strengthening of existing connections, and the pruning of unused connections. It helps build your wisdom and knowledge. Neuroplasticity is essential for learning, memory and recovery from injury and trauma. It has the ability to help change behaviours, responses, and dysfunctional patterns of thinking to develop new mindsets, memories, skills, and new abilities. Hence love-based affirmations, blessings, and breathing exercises!

VIBRATIONS, THOUGHTS, BLESSINGS, AND FEELINGS ALL MAKE A DIFFERENCE

The photos below taken by Emoto are of the same water crystal.

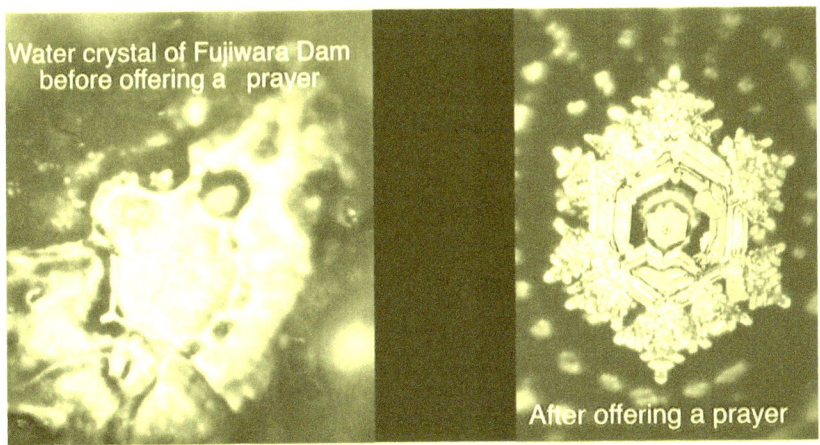

Emoto and others I discovered when studying Feng Shui, also illustrate the effects on the molecular structure of food when cooking with microwaves, sitting too close to the TV, and such. However, Emoto discovered that charging water with <u>gratitude as well as love</u>, gave it an immunity against the microwaves. Fascinating, right?

Does that mean if we charge our bodies each day with gratitude and love, we create an immunity to the toxins and other detrimental chemicals and frequencies in our atmosphere and environment?

It's an experiment worth proving for yourself.

In the past, I encountered resistance to Emoto's ideas when I included them in an article for a water magazine I was editing. Despite being ahead of its time, the article was pulled due to scepticism. However, as science progresses, there is increasing interest in validating soul/spirit-based ideologies, leading to potential breakthroughs that could validate ageless wisdom. It is always an interesting process when proof of ageless wisdom occurs. Imagine the news media announcing the amazing 'breakthroughs' of science? It's already a recurring pattern.

I consistently immerse myself in the highest vibrations of love and gratitude, originally inspired by Louise Hay's teachings, and have shared this approach with my clients. While I advocate for holistic wellness and maintain my own health without medications, I emphasise that activation and realisation are personal responsibilities.

Maintaining ethical practice standards, I always encourage individuals to seek medical advice from their General Practitioner (GP) as needed.

LOVE AND RELATIONSHIPS

Self-Love: Embrace self-love by treating yourself with the same care and compassion you would offer your best friend or child. Recognise your worth, acknowledge strengths and areas for growth, and establish healthy boundaries. Relationship challenges often reflect inner struggles, providing opportunities for personal growth and discovering the gift in every challenge.

By healing and accepting your inner child with love and courage, you can transform all relationships. Stand in your self-love, knowing you are complete and worthy. Cultivate positivity, celebrate achievements, and prioritise your well-being, setting boundaries when necessary. Self-love is a personalised practice aligned with your unique needs and values.

Unconditional Love: Unconditional love is often associated with personal relationships similar to the mother/child relationship and signifies a type of love that is free from conditions or limitations. It is a profound and accepting form of love where one person cares deeply for another without placing expectations or requirements on that love.

Unconditional love accepts individuals for who they are, flaws and all, and persists regardless of mistakes or imperfections. This kind of love is often considered to be enduring, steadfast, and resilient in the face of challenges. It is akin to the self-love of the inner child.

Impersonal Love: Impersonal love typically refers to a type of love that is not directed towards a specific individual but is more generalised or universal. It transcends personal connections and may be expressed towards humanity, nature, or existence as a whole. This form of love involves a sense of interconnectedness and compassion for all beings. Impersonal love can be a selfless and expansive feeling that extends beyond personal relationships, encompassing a broader perspective on life and the world.

In summary, while <u>impersonal love</u> is more about a universal, non-personal connection with all existence, <u>unconditional love</u> is a deep and accepting affection typically directed towards specific individuals, marked by its lack of conditions or expectations.

Both concepts represent powerful expressions of love but differ in their scope and focus. However, without first enabling your <u>self-love,</u> it can be challenging to fully experience and extend unconditional love towards others.

Self-love serves as the foundation upon which unconditional love for others can flourish, as it involves accepting and cherishing yourself without judgment or reservation. By cultivating self-love, you can develop the capacity to offer genuine, unconditional love to others, fostering deeper connections and a greater sense of fulfillment in relationships.

> *"The day will come when you shall know*
> *yourself to be life in all its essence,*
> *in all forms and in and through all planes of existence.*
> *When the world shall grasp this great truth, peace shall reign,*
> *for strife cannot exist between man, his neighbour, his country,*
> *because whom would you destroy but yourself."*
> (Ann Herbstreith)

CHAPTER EIGHT

7 SACRED SECRETS

There are Earthly Laws for keeping the peace.
But why do you think crimes increase?
The Laws get abused and often ignored.
And Earthly Laws can be somewhat flawed.

There are no flaws in the Laws of Nature
No Earthly government for Divine Legislature.
From Natural Laws there is no escape
Only you can nurture your soul's landscape.

HERMES TRISMEGISTUS AND HIS ANCIENT EGYPTIAN AND GREEK TEACHINGS
(Interpreted from *The Kybalion*)

The 'Kybalion' offers a contemporary interpretation of Hermetic teachings, delving into spiritual, metaphysical concepts, and the alchemical practices linked with Hermes Trismegistus. It asserts the profound secrecy surrounding these teachings, passed down since the time of Hermes, the revered ancient sage also known as Thoth in Egyptian mythology. Hermes, known as 'The Master of

Masters' and 'Thrice Great Teacher,' excelled in alchemy, astrology, and philosophy. He authored the influential 'Corpus Hermeticum,' exploring divine nature, the cosmos, and human spiritual evolution. Hermes Trismegistus, a fusion of Greek and Egyptian mythologies, symbolises esoteric knowledge and spiritual enlightenment.

The term 'hermetically sealed' originates from alchemists' practices, influenced by Hermeticism, conducted in enclosed environments to protect against perceived dangers of studying mystical concepts. This term reflects the historical and symbolic connection between Hermeticism, alchemy, and the pursuit of hidden knowledge associated with Hermes Trismegistus.

It's important to maintain your thoughts on high,
So, keep on reading for more reasons why
These words and practices are so profound
For us to turn the world around
To peace and harmony and authentic truth
Paving new ways to nurture our youth
And the highest emotional gamut
of our glorious and most beautiful Planet!

A SUMMARY OF THE 7 SACRED HERMETIC PRINCIPALS OF MENTAL ALCHEMY

"The Principles of Truth are Seven;
he who knows these, understandingly,
possesses the Magic Key before whose touch
all the Doors of the Temple fly open."
(The Kybalion)

These Principles are not separate and isolated but are interconnected and work in harmony to shape an understanding of the cosmos and your place within it. You will note how they relate in the upcoming chapters. In the diagram below, I have attempted to illustrate simplistically the interconnectedness of the constant flow of energies within the Divine Mind and Oneness of the ALL.

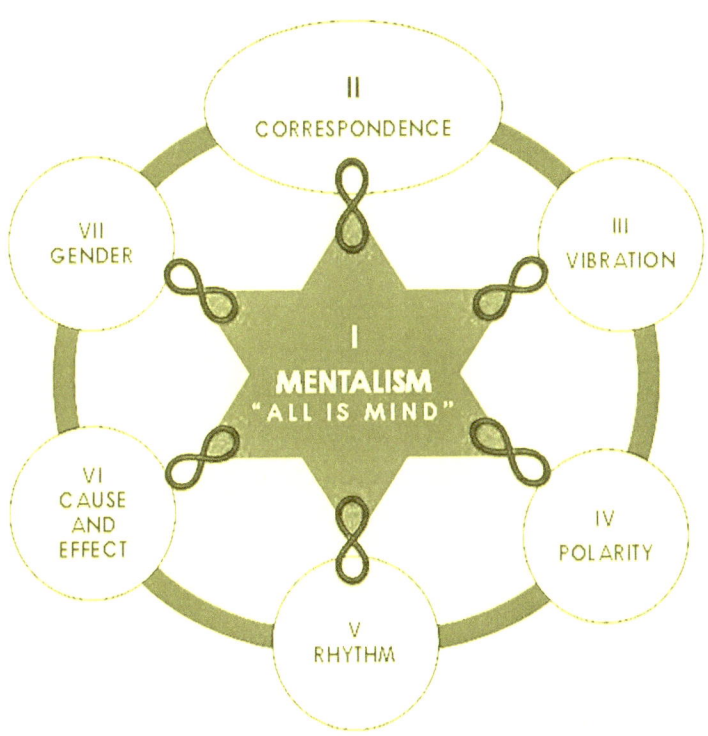

1. **The Principle of Mentalism:**

   "THE ALL IS MIND; the Universe is Mental."
   (The Kybalion)

This Law establishes the fundamental principle that everything originates from the realm of consciousness. Your thoughts and beliefs shape your reality, aligning with the Principle of Cause and Effect. With free choice, you can actively shape your life either constructively or destructively, individually, and collectively. The Divine Mind, the infinite wisdom behind all creation, governs the universe.

As a divine spark of this consciousness, you possess the power to manifest unlimited possibilities through your imagination and superconscious connections. Your inherent magnificence stems from your divine origin as a daughter/son of the Divine Source, embodying the essence of various divine names across cultures.

2. **The Principle of Correspondence:**

"As above, so below; as below, so above."
(The Kybalion)

As Within - So Without
What I see and what you see too
In your outside world,
Is a projection of you.
All bundles of energy correlate
When you master your own
You empower your fate.

Protect what you've learned
And be only concerned
With the goodness and love you can co-create.

The Law of Correspondence demonstrates the interconnectedness between different levels of existence. Understanding the laws governing one plane, will help you understand how the other planes operate.

The patterns and relationships observed in one aspect of life can be reflected in other areas, aligning with the Law of Vibration. Just as different vibrations create different manifestations of thought, form and spirit, the correspondence between different levels and densities of existence gives rise to similar patterns.

This law states that there are consistent patterns and relationships between the various levels of existence; perhaps this resonance is what makes you feel so good after taking a walk in nature.

A point of fascination is how the structure of an atom resembles the structure of our solar system. Electrons orbit around a nucleus, similar to how planets revolve around the sun. This correspondence shows how patterns repeat on different scales, emphasising the interconnectedness of the <u>microcosm and macrocosm</u>.

THE SPIRALLING PATTERNS OF THE COSMOS AND THE FERN FROND

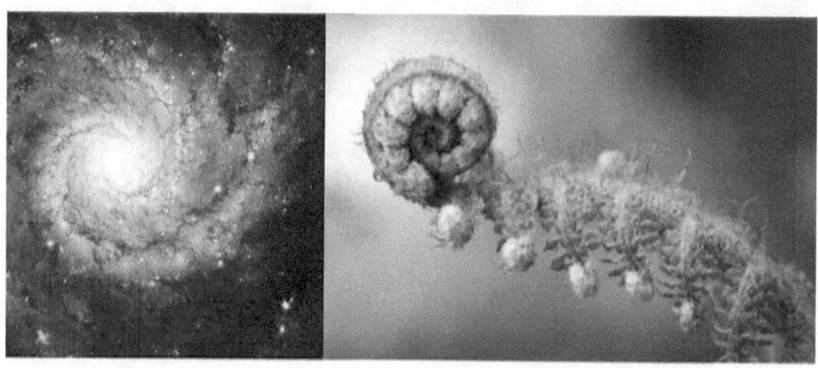

Another fascinating observation is the proton at the nucleus of every atom always has the same fundamental properties regardless of the electrons and neutrons within the atom, which means all atoms have a common denominator.

THE PATTERNS OF THE HUMAN LUNG, TREE BRANCHES AND VEINS

COSMIC CORRESPONDENCE

When delving deep, you discover the 'Oneness' that encompasses all elements, from gases and minerals to plants, animals, and humans, reflecting the potential 'Heavenly' perfection on Earth.

In the current global state of affairs, the egoic influence of humanity is reflected in the delusions of the lower Astral plane which in turn influences the overall well-being of the planet and those earthlings who are untrained in the psycho-spiritual aspects of the mind.

While all other elements of the natural world instinctively follow an upward spiral, perpetuating the continuous process of evolution, <u>human beings, distinguished by our 'unique' cognitive capacities, have disrupted this natural flow through the influence of negative ego</u>.

The unity of 'Oneness' cannot be severed, except within your own consciousness due to a lack of understanding. Through conscious choice, humanity holds dominion over the earth. Creation emanates from the breath of life, forever evolving and spiralling. This universal principle operates in all dimensions of creation. When realisation becomes reality, understanding breaks through in illumination.

3. **The Principle of Vibration:**

   "Nothing rests; everything moves; everything vibrates."
   (The Kybalion)

This Law suggests that everything in the Universe, including thoughts, emotions, and matter, is in a constant state of vibration. Take the example of music. Different musical notes have distinct vibrations and frequencies. When played together, they create either harmonious or dissonant sounds. Colours also vibrate and have an important part to play in harmonising energy fields.

As highlighted, your emotions and thoughts emit vibrations that can affect your well-being and interactions with others. <u>Diverse levels of vibration create different manifestations and experiences</u>. When you hold well-being as the basis of your world, then wellbeing is expressed through your thoughts, emotions, and actions. Wellbeing becomes your natural experience.

This Principle corelates nicely with <u>the Law of Attraction.</u> In this instance *'The Hermetic Art of Mental Alchemy'* deals in the mastery of Mental Forces, or the transmutation of one kind of <u>Mental Vibration</u> into another. The fascinating story regarding the transmutation of material forces and elements will not be addressed in depth in this book! However, suffice to say as everything is in a state of vibration, then this vibration is not arbitrary; it has a rhythm and order that can be manipulated by the infinite possibilities of sentient imagination.

The Kybalion says:

"He who understands the Principle of Vibration has grasped the sceptre of power."

and

"To change your mood or mental state, change your vibration."

4. The Principle of Polarity:

"Everything is Dual; everything has poles; everything has its pair of opposites; like and unlike are the same; opposites are identical in nature, but different in degree; extremes meet; all truths are but half-truths; all paradoxes may be reconciled."
(The Kybalion)

This Principle states that opposites are two extremes of the same energy, and they are necessary for each other to exist. Light and dark, hot, and cold, poverty and wealth are examples of polarities.

Consider the concept of day and night. Daytime represents light and activity, while night-time represents darkness and rest. Both are necessary for the Earth's balance and the well-being of living organisms. This polarity demonstrates how opposing forces coexist and complement each other.

While the Principle of Vibration suggests that everything is in motion, the Principle of Polarity adds the concept that this motion occurs along a spectrum of opposites. Together, they contribute to the understanding of the dynamic and structured nature of the universe.

While negative ego and negative emotions are considered delusional aspects within the natural laws encompassing the entirety of existence, the laws of polarity and vibration offer a pathway to transcend or transmute their chaotic manifestations. For instance, if one experiences the emotion of anxiety, which resides in the realm of negative polarity, efforts can be made to transmute it into serenity, a state aligned with positive polarity.

The transmutation of negative polarity is a process integral to spiritual and personal development. It involves elevating lower or denser aspects to higher vibrations. This conscious practice of transforming negative emotions into positive ones and limiting beliefs into empowering ones, plays a crucial role for those on the path to enlightenment and harmony.

In summarising this transformative journey, it is important to recognise the significance of consciously addressing the only polarity <u>not</u> aligned with natural and divine laws – the polarity of ego.

Understanding that negative ego is an illusion largely created by unconscious conditioning, you can leverage the principle of polarity through heightened awareness and dedicated effort. By doing so, you can tap into your inherent ability to neutralise or transcend these negative aspects.

5. **The Principle of Rhythm:**

    "Everything flows, out and in; everything has its tides."
    (The Kybalion)

This law highlights the rhythmic cycles and patterns that exist in the universe. It explains changes in moods, feelings, and experiences; emphasising that everything has its seasons, and there are fluctuations, ebbs, and flows, in every aspect of life.

Being aware of the principle of rhythm, you are able to watch and recognise what rhythms effect your life negatively and use your higher mind to employ the principles of Polarity, Vibration and Correspondence to overcome them. Thus, neutralising the pendulum swing of ups and downs or higher or lower consciousness through the laws of mentalism. Impersonal love would be considered a neutral polarity.

> *"Rhythm may be neutralised by an application of the Art of Polarisation."*
> (The Kybalion)

6. **The Principle of Cause and Effect:**

> *"Every cause has its effect; every effect has its cause."*
> (The Kybalion)

This principle states that every action produces a corresponding reaction. It highlights the concept of karma and encourages taking responsibility for your choices and their consequence as highlighted throughout this book.

AN EARTHLY/SPIRITUAL EXAMPLE

My garden gave me a bumper crop of tomatoes, spinach, and lettuces this year. There was plenty of sunshine and I planted marigolds alongside the vegetables' to keep the bugs away; the soil was weeded, mulched, nourished and well-watered.

I admit to having talked to the plants often to let them know how beautifully they were growing and how much I appreciated them. Okay, perhaps I went overboard in your eyes, but it worked! There were no bugs on the tomatoes or greens, and because I used pea straw to mulch around the plants, the pea shoots were a surprise to add to my salads, along with the marigold petals – a beautiful effect.

Of course, within the natural cycles and rhythms of life, you can't rest on your laurels; the entire process is a repeat next season.

The point is the conditions were ideal for my vegetables to flourish, which they did. They grew and became their <u>natural potential</u>. They were given care, nourishment, protection, and attention which <u>caused the effect</u> of a happy garden with bumble bees buzzing, no pests, and my summer dining adorned with an abundance of pretty and nourishing salads. The effects were far more than what I had figured in the beginning, providing an abundance of benefits.

THE HOLISITC METAPHOR

In the holistic concept of <u>everyday living</u>, the law of cause and effect extends beyond the tangible realms of gardening to the intricate tapestry of human existence. Just as the garden thrived under the conditions of care, nourishment, protection, and attention, you can consider this principle in the cultivation of your own life. Your actions, choices, and intentions act as seeds planted in the soil of existence, yielding consequences that ripple through the interconnected threads of your experiences.

In the same context, fostering positive relationships, maintaining a healthy lifestyle, and practicing a mindful presence can be likened to the tending of a metaphorical garden. Cultivating emotional well-being, for instance, requires sowing seeds of kindness, empathy, and understanding. The attention given to personal growth, similar to the care bestowed upon the garden, results in the blossoming of your inherent potential.

Just as the gardener must adapt to the changing seasons, as recognised in the Principle of Rhythm, we all must navigate life's natural ebbs and flows. Reflecting on the cause-and-effect dynamics in daily choices, you might recognise that a positive mindset and proactive approach often lead to a cascade of beneficial outcomes. Conversely, neglect or negativity may result in a harvest of challenges.

This perspective emphasises the interconnectedness of various aspects of life, acknowledging that the effects of our actions extend beyond immediate circumstances. Just as the garden's bounty exceeded expectations, embracing a holistic approach to life can yield unexpected and enriching consequences, fostering a sense of fulfillment, resilience, and interconnected well-being.

7. **The Principle of Gender:**

> *"Gender is in everything; everything has its masculine and feminine principles."*
> (The Kybalion)

This principle suggests that gender exists on all levels of creation and is not limited to biological sex. It represents the duality and complementary nature of energy and creation.

Look at the concept of yin and yang. Yin represents feminine energy characterised by qualities such as nurturing, intuition, and receptivity. Yang represents masculine energy associated with qualities like strength, assertiveness, and action.

Both energies exist within everyone and must be synthesised to create harmony. In other words, the feminine principle receives impressions, while the masculine principle tends to give out or express. The Feminine principle therefore has a much more varied field of operation than has the Masculine Principle.

New thoughts, concepts, ideas, including the work of the imagination are generated by the <u>feminine principle</u>. The <u>masculine principle</u> is 'Will' in action in its variety of ways.

A PERSONAL EXAMPLE

Without the harmonious integration of the masculine and feminine principles, this book would have lingered solely within the realms of my imagination for an extended period. Now, by consciously activating the masculine principle, I embark on the active endeavour of transcribing these timeless insights in my distinctive manner. This, I do for the benefit of those discerning individuals like yourself, who choose to engage with and act upon information that may transcend current subjective beliefs.

As the principle of gender aligns in a state of equilibrium and harmony, it summons forth superior forces that collaborate to enhance the unfolding process.

> *There are many dimensions that make up you.*
> *'Though the body you have is temporary too*
> *It's useful for taking the actions required*
> *To realise your goals and the ideas you've inspired.*

SUMMARY

Delving into The Law of Cause and Effect elucidates this intricate dance of cosmic principles. A parallel example manifests in the magnetic forces within the Law of Attraction, drawing forth myriad opportunities that serve as mirrors to gauge your vibrational frequency and pinpoint any lingering resistance within your energy field.

Ultimately, all these laws work together to highlight the interconnectedness, harmony, and balance of the universe. They provide a holistic framework for understanding the nature of reality, consciousness, and personal transformation, allowing you to align your thoughts, actions, and vibrations with the universal principles for a more fulfilling and purposeful life.

By mastering the Mental Art of Alchemy, you can skilfully transmute undesirable elements into those of great worth and, in doing so, achieve triumph. It is imperative to refrain from embracing a form of half-wisdom that, in essence, is folly – a wisdom that neglects the fundamental truth.

The Kybalion highlights that:

"True mastery lies not in indulging in abnormal dreams, fanciful visions, or fantastical imaginings, but rather in harnessing the higher forces to overcome the lower. Escaping the tribulations of the lower planes is achieved by vibrating on the frequencies of the higher realms."

Developing and trusting your higher inner guidance is a practiced skill, vital for transmuting the drama in any given situation and breaking free from negative behavioural patterns accumulated over lifetimes.

When you have found your ideal polarity in a situation, it is vital to employ both the masculine and feminine principles necessary to manifest it.

"Always bear in mind that the weapon of the Master is transmutation, not presumptuous denial; and to employ the imagination of the feminine in harmony with the will and action of the masculine."
(The Kybalion)

CHAPTER NINE

THY WILL BE DONE!

KNOW THYSELF

For centuries, humanity has been urged to 'Know Thyself,' yet exploration has primarily focused on the physical body rather than the whole being. Understanding the multidimensional nature of body, mind, soul, and spirit reveals varying levels of energy vibration, each influenced by the higher or lower mind directing them.

Recognising yourself as an interconnected energy system within a broader network is a leap in consciousness. Working with the Law of Vibration and other natural laws empowers you to command your life and impact your environment positively.

Vibrational Healing emphasises grace over drama, harnessing the innate energies of the 'Covenant of Divine Light' within as the director of these energies:

ASTRAL

THE SACRED TRINITY
PERSONAL POWER - IMPERSONAL LOVE - WISDOM

METAPHORIC MENTAL EXERCISE

Imagine you are part of a humungous great orchestra. You hold a unique instrument that has the ability to keep perfect tune. As you practice using the divine qualities of your unique instrument, every day in every way your music resonates more authentically within and without – above and below. You are aware that there are many around you playing their unique instruments too; and more than a few are way out of tune, causing great discord.

You recognise that they are not as adept at playing their instruments as you are. Many of them are totally unaware of their innate ability to harmonise.

Questions:

1. Do you play your instrument 'out of tune' to make them feel better?
2. Do you play your instrument 'out of tune' because you think you should conform?
OR...
3. Do you hold your divine resonance with love, humility, without judgement, with forgiveness and without attachment to the drama?

EVOLVING YOUR PERSONAL POWER

This Golden Age is the time to step into your personal power; to release yourself from victimhood. When you become aware of all the invisible energies that can affect your life for better or worse (from within and without – from above and below), your personal power can be acted upon with discernment and effect betterment for ALL.

It becomes a journey of service to yourself and your unique purpose first and foremost. Hence the affirmations mentioned.

In the orchestral metaphor above, dissolving your own bad karma contributes to dissolving humanity's karma, aligning with the sacred trinity of POWER, LOVE, and WISDOM. Holding your tune aids others in harmonising, akin to collective meditations fostering peace and healing. These efforts embody impersonal love and co-creative power, aimed at peace and alleviating suffering without attachment to specific outcomes.

> *Being aware of what your mind can do,*
> *Gives you free choice to follow through.*

However, when you use your free choice to choose substances, thoughts and behaviours that have detrimental effects on yourself and others, your bad karma multiplies and causes a downward slope of destruction for yourself and those other powerless unaware individuals who may be keeping your company (and vice versa, of course).

What is good is that my words in this book are channelled to you from the place where all goodness resides. If you resonate, all you have to do is quietly become more authentic in yourself, read on, and reap the benefits of your practice. If you don't resonate, so be it.

The power is in your choice, for you are the one responsible for the effects of your choices.

You are aware now that the question of <u>dissolving karma</u> comes down to how conscious you are of doing what you do. The level and degree of your divinity is within your own <u>thought processes, the choices you make, the actions you take, and the company you keep</u>. As the Master Jesus once said:

"Do unto others as you would have others do unto you."

THE SEARCH FOR WELLNESS

Throughout history, humanity has engaged in an extensive array of experiments, spanning eons, and involving diverse substances, products, learnings, and behaviours; all in search of a sense of serenity, self-worth, and wellness. This pursuit has often diverted attention from individuals' embracing their innate personal power and self-responsibility.

Whether embarking on unprotected ventures into the astral planes, delving deeply into the realms of technology, or exploiting mind-altering substances, both sanctioned and unregulated, you can guarantee there will be trouble afoot if you have not sorted out your own mental disharmony and negative ego primarily.

PRACTICING DISCERNMENT

No one can do your work but you,
No one can carry your cross.
When you recall what you already know,
You start to become your own boss.
And when living from your highest self,
You realise who else gives a toss!

Practicing discernment is an exercise in personal power, crucial for making important life choices. Whether evaluating teachings, group dynamics, or psychic connections, discerning their authenticity and vibrational energy is essential. This book aims to guide you in stepping into your personal power and authenticity with wisdom and discernment. Before aligning with a group, philosophy, or guru, it's vital to discern their alignment with their own authenticity. Similarly, when engaging in psychic connections, discerning between lower astral and higher spiritual planes is crucial. Invoking a protective Golden Egg of swirling God-energy can help safeguard your vulnerabilities in the process. Recognising triggers and removing yourself from overwhelming situations is key to maintaining well-being. The resonance in your heart and your gut are good indicators of discernment.

VULNERABILITIES AND THE NEED TO DE-HYPNOTISE

Humankind has survived (not particularly thrived) through lifetimes of being unconsciously 'hypnotised' into believing some wacky things that are not necessarily true. This statement could be defined as a 'subjective truth.'

Whatever you personally currently believe would be your own subjective truth. The journey through the landscape of the soul is a searching for absolute truth. To progress your ideal inner and outer world, there is a way forward that guarantees your success. However, being willing to discover yourself in all your glory is a necessary component.

PROTECTION AND DETACHED INVOLVEMENT

In search of peace and wellness, it is important to be aware of what is in the way of that and to learn how to practice a 'detached involvement' to both inner and outside destructive influences. Within the Law of Polarity, this could be construed as a 'neutral' position. A neutral position is a position of non-judgement.

> *"We attract what we judge until we
> no longer judge what we attract."*
> (Matt Khan)

THE TEENAGER'S MINDSET

Every one of us is on an evolutionary journey at varying states of consciousness. Frequently, engaging in the array of experiments and behaviours mentioned can serve as a means of <u>temporary escape</u> from a largely <u>faulty three-dimensional mindset</u> of *"Be what you are and do what you want, regardless."*

I compare this mindset to a teenager exploring newfound freedom in search of his or her own identity. Many are unaware that the frontal lobe of the brain does not fully develop until around the age of twenty-four. The frontal lobe is responsible for shaping social behaviour and personal characteristics. It controls things such as personality, decision making, motivation, and voluntary movements.

Before the frontal lobe is fully developed, there is generally no concept of the consequences of actions nor the principle <u>of Cause and Effect</u> which is the basis of responsible 4th dimensional (4D) consciousness.

Most parents unknowingly influence their children through behaviours, emotions, and cultural patterns during the formative years when children are primarily in a theta brain wave state, akin to hypnosis.

In this crucial developmental phase, children absorb and mimic their parents' actions and attitudes, often replicating both positive and negative aspects. This concept likens the dynamic to 'the blind leading the blind' – in some respects, emphasising the inadvertent transmission of patterns from one generation to the next.

"Give me a child until he is seven, and I will give you the man!"

The exact origin of this adage is uncertain; however it is often attributed to the Jesuit's catholic education institutions.

Whether a child rebels or conforms, there is an inherent issue triggering an unconscious quest arising in teenage years, for self-identity and an expression of empowerment. Recognising this dynamic calls for a thoughtful and conscious approach to parenting that goes beyond the surface, aiming to break the cycle of unconscious patterns.

Where does the vicious cycle end?

Conscious parenting refers to the fostering of awareness and intentional guidance during these early years. It is fundamental for the child's healthy growth and well-being. Thankfully, more parents are changing their own ingrained habits and making an impact on the younger generation, which is becoming evident in some areas, but definitely not in general.

ASTRAL

ESCAPISM

Addictions can spring from a perceived need to escape from the illusory inner demons spawned by an unconscious mindset entwined with distorted beliefs. These intricate constructs may arise from skewed patterns of negative self-image stemming from unresolved emotional reactions and infantile needs that have not been met. Addictions of course, perpetuate the cycle of destruction which feeds the pockets of the unscrupulous.

The need for **escapism** can also be influenced by genetic and DNA factors or unresolved challenges carried over from past lives. Even the transition from earlier states of consciousness where instinct and habits were survival; or security was assured by the elders, tribal customs, and a connection to nature and spiritual ancestors. Evolving into three-dimensional consciousness (or the next rung up) can be a challenging and insecure time.

There is no quick fix, pill, plant, drink, technology, or drug, that can dissolve your karma, cure your illness, or take your consciousness to Utopia, and keep you there in an integrated, harmonious, and healthy way. I have known plenty who have tried by these means; and suffered disastrous consequences, destroying relationships, health, and families along the way (an unconscious trail of destruction).

Fortunately for some, this 'dark night of the soul' eventually inspires more spiritual choices.

ALCOHOLISM AND DRUGS

The consumption of alcohol has significant repercussions on the human psyche, with its impact extending beyond mere intoxication.

When individuals indulge in alcohol, the critical and conscious mind is subdued, allowing the subconscious mind to take control. Alarmingly, the prevalence of alcoholism is on the rise, and the age at which people engage in alcohol consumption is decreasing, particularly among high school and college students. What may initially begin as a source of weekend entertainment often spirals into addiction, acting as a gateway to other forms of substance abuse and becoming a fast track to personal destruction.

Despite the widely recognised and disastrous effects linked with alcohol, its consumption persists as a normalised aspect of society, fostered through informal advertising in films, events, celebrations, and the influence of role models. Alcohol commercials flood numerous media outlets, liquor stores are pervasive, and those involved in its production and sale often prioritise profit over ethical considerations, figuratively 'selling their souls to the devil'.

This widespread presence further contributes to the escalating issue. In contrast, drug pedlars operate with more subversiveness in their exploitation, adding to the complexity of the problem.

Beyond the immediate physical and psychological toll, both alcohol consumption and mind altering substances are noted for creating vulnerabilities in the individual's aura, leading to not only psychological numbness but also the degradation of the physical body. The impact extends even beyond the physical realm, as astral entities, once addicts in their earthly existence, may persist in their addiction on the emotional plane after passing to the astral world.

These entities may energetically engage with individuals who are addicted to alcohol, participating in a kind of ethereal celebration through their host's experiences and subsequently influencing their earthly behaviours and health.

The sobering reality is that if alcoholics and drug addicts were to witness how astral entities exploit their addiction and bodies for their own ethereal 'parties,' they would be appalled. This phenomenon serves as a poignant indicator of a planet that is characterised by backwardness and spiritual immaturity.

Alcoholism within my own family has been just one of the many drivers for my delving into the spiritual psychology of the mind, and indeed for authoring this book. It is vitally important to recognise the manipulation of the marketplace in this regard; and to develop your intuition or discernment in making your own life changing choices.

'POWER-OVER' THE POWERLESS: 3D CONSCIOUSNESS

The promotion of harmful substances and behaviours, driven by profit motives reveals a disturbing agenda of immediate gain without compassion. Fear mongers, whether intentional or unintentional, contribute to chaos, highlighting the need for education on subtle energies. Exploiting vulnerabilities for escapism or relief reflects a 'power-over' mentality, symptomatic of the manipulators' projected "powerlessness" demonstrating a three-dimensional consciousness focused on material identity.

Extreme examples like communism and various forms of abuse showcase power imbalances, contrasting with acts of compassion such as overthrowing dictators and aiding the vulnerable. These actions don't empower individuals but rather reflect powerlessness projected onto others.

However, not all operate from this selfish perspective. Transcending it involves utilising imagination and aligning with ideals of higher consciousness. Fourth dimensional consciousness is responsibly living the Law of Cause and Effect actively.

The evident manifestations of our worldwide mental health crises starkly illustrate the far-reaching fallout stemming from these distorted mindsets.

Take a breath!

A 'detached involvement' is what you need here.
As you become more aware of the exploitations of fear
Think to yourself of all that is dear!
Seek the love in your heart, it's forever there.
Know all bad motives are far from God's Truth
They are actions created by the shrewdly uncouth.
Connect to the love that inspires your soul.
You will add to the light that heals the WHOLE.
To bury your head is a dangerous game
Unless you want everything to stay the same!

WRAPPING UP EXPLOITATION

As substances, products and behaviours are glamorised or glamorously packaged, they may appear as quick fixes or appealing alternatives, further enticing those grappling with emotional turmoil, stress, or societal pressures.

Consequently, the widespread prevalence of economic, mental, and physical health issues in our global society can be seen as a testament to the distorted thinking, toxicity and behavioural patterns that are perpetuated and amplified by such strategies.

ASTRAL

STANDING IN PERSONAL POWER

Trigger #111 prompted me to speak out at conference to emphasise the importance of energy protection. I assumed the presenter knew this, but assumptions can lead to misunderstandings. Had he been aware of the emotional and mental dimensions, he might have understood better. My acting on earlier signs could have prevented his humiliation, but the outcome led to writing this book, for which I'm grateful.

The kick in the gut: How often have you felt that gut-wrenching sensation? It takes courage to confront it and harness your innate power. You're not a victim of others' actions or your own inner turmoil. You hold the reins to your thoughts, emotions, and choices, paving the way for your well-being.

Staying true to yourself amid life's twists and turns empowers you to act from wisdom and love. Seek guidance when needed; it's honourable to do so. In conflicts, recognise projection and choose kindness over ego-driven reactions. Abuse is never love; prioritise self-respect and seek support when necessary. Egoic games aren't just personal; they manifest in global systems, fuelling power struggles, competition, and division. Resistance to change drains you; embrace growth instead.

<u>Global exploitation is entrenched in our society. However, it would not exist if we each individually took responsibility for educating and nurturing ourselves wisely in self-love and self-empowerment. At a soul level we can use our innate intuition to turn all knowledge into wise action and make positive change.</u>

Recognising your innate uniqueness empowers you to confront any challenge with confidence. When you stand authentically in your personal power, you're liberated from concern over others' opinions or actions. You can observe your own reactions, sense them inwardly, and respond wisely, remaining calm amidst the chaos unfolding around you. You possess the capability to be the calm centre amidst the storm.

*Spirit is something you generally can't see.
It is the connection of love between you and me.
It's the thoughts you think that make you glad.
Through the soul to the spirit of your mighty monad.*

As a trusting individual, I've faced exploitation in life, prompting me to become more discerning. Each challenge is an opportunity for growth, recurring until we learn its lesson. Mastery of personal power isn't about control over others; it's about inner strength and empowerment. Standing in your power means embracing authenticity, wisdom, and resilience, regardless of physical condition. Maintaining mental strength is crucial, even amidst exhaustion. Nourishing the mind with spiritual practice is as vital as caring for the body.

Discernment and awareness are the initial steps; addressing systemic challenges requires a collaborative effort involving various stakeholders like parents, therapists, educators, communities, and organisations.

*There is potential good and bad in everyone.
It is the choices you make that can heal or destroy.*

It is crucial to <u>shed light</u> on deceptive negative ego practices. This is to empower you to recognise and safeguard yourself against potential exploitation; and to encourage personal empowerment. It also enlists the invisible world of your soul to give you encouragement and fortitude in your life's journey.

NATURAL LAW MEETS TRADITIONAL PSYCHOLOGY

The Natural Law of <u>Cause and Effect</u> relates to the traditional psychological analysis that *"through conflict comes growth, understanding, and the potential for positive change."*

Conflict can be a catalyst for learning from different perspectives, challenging existing beliefs, and fostering empathy and compassion. When handled constructively, conflict can lead to stronger relationships, improved communication, and the resolution of underlying issues.

It provides an opportunity for individuals and groups to collaborate, find common ground, and work towards shared goals. By embracing conflict with openness and a willingness to learn, you can harness its transformative power and use it as a steppingstone to progress your wisdom and personal development.

DEMONSTRATIONS OF EARTHLY PERSONAL POWER

Self-awareness: Knowing your strengths, weaknesses, values, and desires, fostering self-love and authenticity.
Self-confidence with humility: Believing in yourself while remaining open to learning and growth.
Self-discipline: Exerting control over impulses and consistently pursuing goals.
Emotional intelligence: Understanding and managing your own emotions while respecting others' feelings.
Resilience: Bouncing back from setbacks and using challenges as opportunities for growth.
Assertiveness: Expressing opinions and boundaries confidently yet respectfully.

Adaptability: Embracing change and learning from experiences.
Goal setting: Clearly defining objectives and working systematically toward them.
Communication skills: Effectively articulating thoughts and emotions with respect and detachment.
Empowering others: Lifting others up and creating positive impacts on the community.
Humility: Recognising your worth, while treating others with respect and care, prioritising the well-being of all.

There is no other way to fashion your own world, but through the creations and imaginations of your own mind.

How can you live in an enlightened mind, if you give your personal power away to endarkened minds and distorted beliefs?

SUMMARY

When you view the above scenarios with a clear mind, you will see the lack of personal power and love displayed across the whole spectrum.

The outward expression of powerlessness is anger in all its guises.

The inward expression of powerlessness is anger turned inwards which can embody itself as dis-eases such as cancer.

On one hand, the producers of destructive or inane products could be considered manipulators with some understanding of the human psyche. Why?

Usually for monetary gain, and a lack of conscience; frequently under the guise of a helping hand, but with no higher ethics or values to back them up. In effect, these are groups and systems expressing their own powerlessness by taking power over others. The scenarios are endless.

Of course, that is not to say that all groups are endarkened. As you work through your own inner wisdom and that of this book, you will develop your own intuitive abilities more, so you can identify who/what is supportive to your higher good and who/what is not.

It's never too late to change your fate!

Question: If you are a user of mind-altering substances, behave badly, have lost your passion, have negative thoughts and feelings, are a bully or control freak, who/what are you giving your personal power away to? Is it the producer, the marketer, the manipulator, the bully, the parent, the cause, the reactions, or the substance?

Answer: Despite what you have been through, you are not a victim. All those challenges have presented an opportunity for you to find the gift in them. There is no one else to blame for your own thoughts, feelings, behaviours, and reactions. **There is a gift to be had in the awareness of that**. It is never too late to forgive yourself and others, to let go of old stuff and move on in your power and wisdom.

"Through guidance and process Ascended Mastery is achievable by Self-Conscious effort; it requires a re-generation from within of enough unconditional Love, Light, Power and Wisdom to snap the chains of all human limitation, and so stand Ascended and Free, and worthy to be trusted with the use of creative forces beyond those of normal human experience."
(St Germaine)

CHAPTER TEN

THE POINT OF EQUILIBRIUM

DISCERNMENT AND DISCRIMINATION

Using your power of spiritual discernment based on impersonal love is a beautiful tool to discriminate what is authentic in all the information that comes your way. Your gut and your heart will let you know the feeling of its authenticity or not.

You can also examine the principle of polarity and embrace the concept of detached involvement or neutrality. Consider the interdependence of chaos and order. They are inseparable, each requiring the presence of the other for existence.

Begin by understanding your own position and identifying where you currently stand. Seek the neutral standpoint, that point of equilibrium similar to the space between an inhale and exhale. From this balanced vantage point, you gain the ability to shape circumstances in any desired manner.

Avoid passing judgment, as deeming something as 'bad' aligns you with that negativity automatically. Instead, view situations from a neutral perspective, fostering a safe and unbiased position.

From this standpoint, you can initiate transformation, turning the situation into a positive outcome. While you are on your soul journey to more easy discernment, here is a basic logical earthly aid.

CONSCIOUS <u>LOGICAL</u> ON THE SPOT DISCERNMENT

Be prepared for 'on-the-spot discernment.' Making quick decisions in the moment can be challenging but is often necessary in various situations. Here are some tips for quick logical discernment. Remember, your initial gut reaction can often provide valuable insights.

1. **Prioritise Core Values**: Have a clear understanding of your core values. When faced with a decision, consider whether the options align with your fundamental principles.
2. **Breathe and Centre Yourself**: Take a moment to breathe deeply and centre yourself. This can help calm your mind and allow your intuition to come forward.
3. **Consider Consequences**: Quickly assess potential consequences of each option. Consider short-term and long-term effects on yourself and others. Ideally have a win-win in mind.
4. **Focus on the Essentials**: Identify the key factors or criteria that matter most in the situation. This can help you cut through complexity and make a more streamlined decision.
5. **Listen to Your Body**: Pay attention to physical sensations. If you feel tension or discomfort, it might be a sign that something is off. If you feel a sense of ease, it is usually an indication that the decision is in alignment.
6. **Ask Clarifying Questions**: If possible, ask quick clarifying questions to gather more information. This can provide a clearer picture and aid in decision-making.

7. **Set Boundaries:** Know your limits and be willing to set boundaries. Sometimes, saying 'no' or taking a step back is the best decision, even in the heat of the moment.
8. **Visualise Outcomes while Embracing Flexibility**: Quickly visualise potential outcomes of each choice.

Trust the images and feelings that come up during this mental exercise. Understand that not all decisions need to be final. Sometimes, making a preliminary decision and staying open to adjustments based on new information is a valid approach. 'On-the-spot' discernment improves with practice.

Over time, you will become more attuned to your instincts and superconscious spiritual guidance, and be better equipped to make quick, effective decisions. Additionally, learn from your experiences to refine your ability to discern in the moment.

UNCONSCIOUS DISCERNMENT: THE ARM TEST

You will need a partner to assist here.

Another method used to access information from the body's energy system is called the 'arm test.' Here is a simple way to perform it for discernment.

Establish a baseline: Stand comfortably with your feet shoulder-width apart. Extend one arm straight out to the side at shoulder height, parallel to the ground. This arm will be your indicator. Breathe in the golden sea of light.

1. **Ask a clear question**: Clearly formulate a question in your mind related to the decision or situation you're seeking discernment about. Ensure the question has a 'yes' or 'no' answer.
2. **Test for a positive response**: With your arm extended, have someone gently press down on your wrist while you resist the pressure. You should be able to maintain strong resistance. This is considered a 'positive' response.
3. **Test for a negative response**: Now, think of a statement that is opposite to what you want to hear or a 'no' response. Again, have someone press down on your wrist while you resist. If your arm weakens or drops, this is considered a 'negative' response.
4. **Repeat for confirmation**: Repeat the process with different questions or statements to confirm the consistency of the responses.

Experiment:

- Hold a packet of sugar or some highly processed food in the opposite hand to the arm you are holding out; and ask the question is this good for me? Note the result.
- Now replace the sugar with a piece of organic fruit or vegetable and ask the same question. Note the result.

The effectiveness of any technique can vary among individuals. Interpretation requires practice and a clear understanding of your own body's responses. Some people find success with this method, while others may not resonate with it.

THE POINT OF EQUILIBRIUM

MUSCLE TESTING WITH THE ASSISTANCE OF YOUR OWN DIVINITY

There are varying ways to connect with your higher self to help you discern. It becomes natural with practice. What works for some, may not work for others, however.

I encourage you to test different techniques to find which suits you best. These exercises access your subconscious mind through your muscles. However, you can employ the higher spiritual dimensions within to help you attain more accuracy.

Always approach these techniques with an open mind and a light heart and use them as one of many tools for discernment. These exercises are not intended to be used as means for making every life decision; but they are fun to practice while connecting with your higher dimensions.

Preparation and Divine Inspiration for Authentic Answers:

1. Find a quiet space with no distractions where you can be comfortable.
2. Ask the imaginings of your unconscious and your superconscious mind to assist:

Alternatively, you can call forth the assistance of one or all of the following by name: God, Adonai, Buddha, Allah, Maitreya, Melchizedek, The Mahatma, Jesus Christ, the Holy Spirit, your guardian angels, Archangel Michael; or any number of millions of enlightened Spiritual Beings that are the 'God-Force' in Service to the Divine Plan.

ASTRAL

These Supreme Beings of eternal love and goodness are within the matrix of energy that exists within the Heavenly Dimensions, vibrations, and colourful energy that is your Mighty I AM presence. It is easier to employ the energy and help of those parts of you that are not grappling with earthly egoic challenges.

3. Imagine a silver cord of light grounding you to the centre of the earth.
4. Close your eyes while you call forth God's swirling Golden Egg of Protection.
5. Take a couple of long full breaths into your heart and into your gut, and smile.
6. Open your eyes and begin your exercise.

The Pendulum is a Tool of the Unconscious:

When you are starting out, it's fun for some to use a pendulum to invoke 'yes/no;' 'true/false;' 'good/bad' or 'I don't know' answers to discern what is positive or not in your field of energy.

If you can hold your thoughts in a neutral spot when you are practicing, your all-knowing self through you muscle responses will support more accurate results within the swing of the pendulum.

> *Hold the pendulum steady as it hangs from your hand*
> *Keep yourself still while you upright stand.*
> *First ask the pendulum to give you a 'YES.'*
> *Allow the pendulum to do the rest.*
>
> *It could go into a spin, or it may well swing.*
> *Just Let it do its very own thing.*
> *When you are clear that 'YES' is shown.*
> *Steady it again, for the 'Nos' to be known.*

THE POINT OF EQUILIBRIUM

Make a mental note of which one is which.
(You can ask for a 'don't know' to avoid any glitch).

When you have your swings and spins
Test your discernment,
While you're still on your pins.

Is my name Pamm? I ask it now.
It swings for 'Yes.' Do you wonder how?
Your muscles know what is true for you.
When logic doesn't influence what they want to do.

When God and the Angels are invited to play,
Your glorious answers will show you the way.
Depending on the way they sway,
You can make ideal choices every day!

Another test just for fun
(I promise just another one!)
Is this book worth reading? I ask once more.
Another 'YES.' What a great encore!

THE BODY SWAY

This can be done alone; but you can also ask help from your guardian angels.

1. Stand comfortably with your feet shoulder-width apart; put your mind to its neutral mode and follow the same instructions as for the pendulum.
2. However, this time, allow your body to sway back or forward to give you the answers 'yes' or 'no.'

3. If you want a 'don't know' the body sometimes swings from side to side or to-and-fro fairly rapidly. Test it out and find out what is right for you. Again keep your mind out of the equation.
4. Notice the results.

Each time you use any one of these methods on separate occasions, you will need to start from step one.

CHAPTER ELEVEN

ENERGETIC YOU

CHAKRAS

There are seven main chakras interrelated with your physical being; and many more within the light bodies of your spiritual presence. Chakra is a Sanskrit word for the wheels or discs of subtle spinning energy that must be open and free to allow the wisdom of the ages to awaken within you, little by little according to law. Remember, you cannot take Heaven by storm.

Chakras are attached to the physical through the central nervous, hormonal, and endocrine systems and can be influenced or become clogged by negative states (emotions, thoughts, and memories). Harmonious balancing of the chakras is essential for wellbeing, wholeness, health, and higher spiritual connection.

Chakras are the main centres of energy through which your life force must flow freely. For the purpose of this book, I am focusing on the unintegrated first three lower chakras of earthly living that manipulative behaviours and negative emotions relate to and can influence greatly. A huge percentage of the world population is stuck in the first three chakras – which relate to physical, emotional, and mental development and balance.

Knowledge and awareness are essential for harmonising all chakras. However, a little knowledge can be a dangerous thing. Wise reasoning must be applied to climb the ladder from the lowest chakra of animal nature to the Crown Chakra which brings the illumination that comes with the wisdom and understanding of the higher vibrational realms within.

THE FIRST 3 CHAKRAS DEALING WITH EARTHLY LIVING

I shall delve a bit deeper into the first three chakras, as they often serve as the focal points for individuals encountering blockages that can manifest as physical ailments when the emotional component is not addressed promptly. While I will not extensively explore this topic here, it is crucial to acknowledge how these blocked or disharmonious chakras can impact your physical well-being. This expansive topic yields many insightful narratives in the realm of energy healing.

For instance, prostate cancer may be linked to energetic stagnation or blockages in the first and second chakras, underlining the potential correlation between physical health and emotional or spiritual imbalances. Among men, lower chakra challenges often stem from an excessive focus on the sexual aspects of life rather than leading from the heart centre. Similarly, women's issues like ovarian or uterine cancer may also be tied to energetic imbalances or blockages in these foundational chakras.

These conditions, among others, can be influenced by a variety of factors, including experiences of abuse, abortions, as well as psychological and spiritual elements such as past traumas and beliefs carried over from previous lives (refer to the 'sins of the fathers' paragraph).

1. **BASE KUNDALINI OR ROOT CHAKRA** (Muladhara):
   (Base of the spine – red in colour - connected with the sex glands)
   "I am in touch with the Earth. My roots."

   <u>Seat of the Physical</u>: Security and survival. Life force - contains the primary cells that have all of the knowledge of creation and remain the only cells in your body that do not change in your lifetime. The root chakra grounds us in the physical world. *"I AM safe and secure."*

   - Security and survival
   - Control of appetites
   - Grounding
   - Control of five senses
   - Mastery of addictions and bad habits
   - Mastery of Earth energies
   - Proper Mastery and relationship to sexuality
   - Mastery of Money
   - Demonstrating God on Earth
   - Proper care of physical body
   - Manifesting spiritual mission on earth
   - Leaving legacy on earth
   - Fulfilling spiritual contract on earth
   - Manifesting Heaven on Earth
   - Resonates to the note 'C'
   - Black Onyx Obsidian

Effect of Negative Ego Consciousness:

Underactivity: Overly focused on survival, not enough money to pay bills, homelessness. Unfocused on spiritual life and service, just making it through. Earth life and surviving becomes focus. Being afraid of change.
Overactivity: Overly materialistic, too focused on money and business, improper diet, too focused on earthly life. Too caught up in enjoyments and pleasures of earth life. Too grounded to the point of being disconnected from spirit.
Physical embodiments of disharmony interrelate with the bowels and sexual glands.
Harmonising: Get earthly aspect together so you can focus on higher spiritual pursuits, taking care of Physical Body, and developing mastery of prosperity consciousness.

2. **SACRAL OR SEXUAL CHAKRA** (Swadhishtana):
   (Spleen, just beneath the navel – orange in colour - connected with the Leydig gland and the reproductive organs)
   "I AM a Creative Being."

   Seat of Polarity: Was regarded by Edgar Cayce to be the *"seat of the soul."* The balance of masculine and feminine; creativity; sexual energies; passions; reproduction. The back of this chakra relates to the seat of the subconscious.
   As an expression of the ALL, the inheritance of the seven cardinal sins, the genes of the forefathers link to the mass consciousness of misuse of this centre of force which strives for outward expression.

   - Creativity and sexual energy
   - Emotions, feelings, and relationships
   - Pleasure and enjoyment of life

- Passion and desire
- Personal power and confidence
- Connection to others and the world around you
- Healthy boundaries
- Flow and adaptability
- Resonates to Note 'D'
- Carnelian

Effect of Negative Ego Consciousness:

Underactivity: Lack of creativity and passion, emotional numbness, fear of intimacy, low libido, feeling disconnected from emotions and others.
Overactivity: Emotional instability, addiction to pleasure, overly dramatic or sexual behaviour, inability to maintain healthy boundaries, co-dependency.
Physical embodiments of disharmony interrelate with sexual, or reproductive problems.
<u>Harmonising</u>: Cultivating healthy emotional expression, fostering creativity and passion in balanced ways, establishing, and maintaining boundaries in relationships.

3. SOLAR PLEXUS (Manipura):

(Above naval – yellow in colour - connected with the adrenal glands – the sympathetic nervous system found behind the stomach - the pit of the stomach)
"I believe in myself."

<u>Seat of knowledge and History – The Wisdom of the Ages</u>:
This great sleeping giant gives a sense of <u>balance and personal power</u> in the world. When awakened within, then memory of who and what you are will prevail.

- Personal power and self-esteem
- Willpower and confidence
- Digestion and metabolism
- Inner strength and courage
- Emotional balance
- Sense of self-worth and identity
- Transformation and personal growth
- Resonates to Note 'E'
- Citrine

Effect of Negative Ego Consciousness:

Underactivity: Low self-esteem, lack of confidence, feeling powerless, digestive issues, indecision, passive behaviour, victimhood, frustration.

Overactivity: Domineering or controlling behaviour, excessive competitiveness, aggression, perfectionism, digestive problems, ego-driven actions, anger.

Physical embodiments of disharmony interrelate with gut issues.

Harmonising: Cultivating self-confidence and self-worth, practicing assertiveness without aggression, balancing personal power with humility, promoting healthy digestion and metabolism.

FIRST FOUR HIGHER SELF CHAKRAS

Moving beyond these foundational chakras, the higher chakras, from the heart centre to the crown, play a significant role also. For instance, if self-love is not present and not dealt with, issues around the heart can arise. Physical conditions can corelate to the higher chakras as well and indicate areas of spiritual psychology counselling to focus upon.

4. **HEART CHAKRA (Anahata)**
   (Centre of the chest – green in colour – connected with the thymus gland)
   "I give and receive love."

5. **THROAT CHAKRA** (Vishuddha)
   (Throat area – blue in colour – connected with thyroid gland)
   "I speak my Truth."

6. **THIRD EYE CHAKR**A (Ajna)
   (Between the eyebrows in the centre of the forehead – indigo in colour –connected with pituitary gland)
   "I see clearly."

7. **CROWN CHAKRA**(Sahasrara)
   (The top of the head – violet in colour – sometimes platinum gold, or pure white)
   "I Believe, or I Know."

AN ESSAY ON THE CHAKRAS
By El Morya

As man begins to evolve, he is not aware of the greatness, or wonder of this temple body in which he dwells. And so, very much like the animal, he lives in his five senses, thinking he must earn his living by the 'sweat of the brow'. Indeed, in that state, it is his lot, for the **ROOT CHAKRA** is the only centre awakened in that state.

Now as he begins to evolve, or rise in consciousness, his spleen begins to open. This draws in forces of a higher nature, and he, man, begins to think, *"Who am I?"* or begins his search. This leads him to the seat of Wisdom, the **SOLAR PLEXUS**, and as he seeks or questions, so must this Wisdom respond, for it is all within this wonderfully made body, which contains all the Wisdom of the Ages.

And why, or how could it be otherwise? In the Beginning, man knew himself to be a divine being, a son of God, containing all light, or wisdom. This wisdom he took with him as he descended into matter, or as the search begins, it begins to unravel or unroll the Scroll of his life-pattern. You cannot gain wisdom from outside of yourself. It can only come or be brought to remembrance as: when you hear some truth uttered, you feel this truth. And if another does not feel this as truth, so he rejects it. But Truth is, was, and ever shall be to each, only if, and when it is truth for him.

Now this 'wonderfully made' body temple, the House of the Lord in which 'I' dwell in all My Splendour, or Splenic power, or Radiance. Within this house is the kingdom. Within these centres is contained the ALL, and yet the ALL remains the ALL-ness. Can you comprehend this? Each centre has its own function, and yet all must function in harmony if the body is to be whole.

Now let us discuss the **Solar Plexus**, the seat of wisdom, discerning faculty. This centre reacts to a given action, never errs, therefore it is your guiding light, your discerner. Be not misled for this centre never errs, for it shall always be true to itself. Without this centre man would be a robot, following every indication of another. So, give thanks for this Jewel. It is one that is 'beyond price.':

Now we come to the **HEART**, the Love centre. This shining jewel can easily lead you astray if not ruled wisely. Emotions play upon this vital organ each moment that you live. O, it is well to love, but love impartially, or love all. It is well to sympathise, but if you pour your sympathy upon one already grieved, you pour oil on the fire. Be strong! Give of your light, love, and know that grief is a purifier and must burn itself out. And so, watch your emotions. Do not let them run away with you. Direct, always, in all ways, the love that is you. There is a difference. Impersonal love is not a selfish, but selfless love. Ponder this.

Now we come to the **THROAT** centre, or jewel. *"The word has been placed in thy mouth,"* sang the psalmist, and indeed it is so. The power in this centre can move mountains if used. In declaring the Word, or command it must be just that, a command, knowing it must be obeyed. This is man's heritage. Therefore, speak the Word for what you want. Do not accept every negation that comes upon you, or to you. Praise God for this gift, or jewel.

The next centre is the **PITUITARY**. Its function is to carry all messages to the brain, to awaken the process of illumination, or opening of these centres.

The **PINEAL GLAND** reacts, e.g., or these two glands act and react until in complete agreement. Or, when all questioning ceases and knowing is, these centres join forces and combine in a flash of Light, resulting in the opening of the Lotus, or **CROWN CHAKRA**.

Now all this is according to law of evolution. Man is rewarded according to his search. You see, if he spends all his waking hours pondering truths, asking, delving, it must bring illumination because it is law: as you seek, so shall you find. It is not wise to dwell too long on any aspect of life for to do so creates unbalance, and you must always strive for balance. If in meditation you feel ecstasy, then upon the return you find your daily work which must be done.

And so, give thanks for your wonderfully made body temple. It is the House of the Lord.

SUPPLICATION TO YOUR HIGHEST CONSCIOUSNESS

Supplication refers to the action of earnestly and humbly asking for something, typically in the form of a prayer or a request made to a higher power, such as a deity or God. It often implies a sense of humility, reverence, and sincerity in seeking help, guidance, or blessings.

A poignant observation that the recitation of the Lord's Prayer, for instance, <u>often becomes a rote exercise</u>, devoid of deeper contemplation of its profound implications. In moments like funerals, weddings, or religious gatherings, it's recited almost mechanically, lacking the depth of understanding and reflection it truly deserves.

Yet, the prayer encapsulates essential teachings and principles for leading a meaningful, spiritually rich life. Its words invite introspection, urging individuals to align their will with divine purpose, seek forgiveness and reconciliation, and resist the allure of temptation.

However, the hurried recitation without genuine comprehension overlooks its potential to guide individuals towards holistic living and ethical conduct. Truly embracing the Lord's Prayer entails not just the utterance of its words but an earnest engagement with its message, fostering a deeper connection to spirituality and a more profound sense of purpose in daily existence.

In fact, it melds the messages within the Sacred Laws outlined in this book. The word **'Lord'** often represents a figure of divine authority or sovereignty, while **'Law'** signifies not only human-made regulations but also the Sacred Laws and Principles of Nature, reflecting the correlation between divine authority and the inherent moral guidance found within the natural order. This understanding invites individuals to connect deeply with spirituality and develop a more profound sense of purpose in daily existence, guided by the eternal principles embedded within the fabric of the universe.

The Lord's Prayer

Our Father, who art in heaven,
Hallowed be thy Name.
Thy kingdom come.
Thy Will be done,
On earth as it is in heaven.
Give us this day our daily bread.
And forgive us our trespasses,
As we forgive those who trespass against us.
Lead us away from temptation,
And deliver us from evil.
For thine is the kingdom,
The power, and the glory,
For ever and ever.
Amen.

Consider the 'Invocation'

"**Our Father**" signifies the relationship of humanity with the Divine, acknowledging powerful, caring, and nurturing qualities incorporating both the masculine and feminine principles.

"**Who art in heaven**" acknowledges the transcendence and omnipresence of God, existing beyond earthly limitations and in a realm of divine perfection.

"**Hallowed**" means holy or sacred, indicating reverence and respect for the Divine Essence of our existence.

"**Thy Name**" refers to the identity and essence of God, the Source of All, suggesting that it should be honoured and held in the highest esteem.

"**Thy kingdom come**" expresses a desire for the manifestation of God's reign and divine order on earth, implying the fulfillment and harmony of spiritual and moral ideals in human society.

"**Thy will be done, on earth as it is in Heaven**" emphasises surrendering to the divine Will, aligning human desires and actions with the divine purpose, both in the earthly realm and in the heavenly realm of perfection.

"**Give us this day our daily bread**" – beyond a literal request for sustenance, this line symbolises dependence on God's natural order of abundance for daily provisions, encompassing physical, mental, emotional, and spiritual nourishment.

"**And forgive us our trespasses, as we forgive those who trespass against us**" acknowledges human fallibility and the need for divine forgiveness, while also highlighting the importance of extending forgiveness to self and others, fostering reconciliation and healing.

"**Lead us away from temptation**" acknowledges human vulnerability to temptation and asks for divine guidance and protection against moral and spiritual pitfalls.

"**And deliver us from evil**" is a plea for liberation from the forces of darkness, sin, and suffering, seeking divine intervention to overcome adversity and achieve spiritual wholeness.

"For thine is the kingdom, the power, and the glory, for ever and ever" – this closing line reaffirms the sovereignty and majesty of God, the source of ALL, acknowledging divine authority and eternal presence, inspiring the awe, and reverence that is our inheritance.

"Amen" is a declaration of affirmation and agreement, sealing the prayer with a sense of certainty and faith in the divine.

Breaking down the Lord's Prayer in this manner reveals its depth and richness, offering insights into humanity's relationship with the inner divine nature and providing guidance for living a spiritually fulfilling life.

While the primary context for the Lord's Prayer is for spiritual enlightenment, its profound and universal themes of forgiveness, gratitude, and divine guidance sometimes lead to its use in broader cultural or secular settings.

Here are a few examples where the habit of reciting the Lord's Prayer can sometimes become a perfunctory gesture, detached from its original intent of invoking divine guidance and spiritual reflection – instead serving more as a tradition or formality devoid of genuine connection to its profound message:

Civic Events: In some cultures, or communities, the Lord's Prayer might be recited at civic events, such as public ceremonies, gatherings, or memorials, where there may have been an original desire to invoke a sense of unity, reflection, or reverence.

Educational Settings: In certain educational institutions, particularly those with religious affiliations or traditions, the Lord's Prayer might be recited during assemblies or gatherings as a way to instil moral or spiritual values among students.

ASTRAL

Literary or Cultural References: The Lord's Prayer is sometimes referenced or recited in literature, films, or other forms of art as a symbolic or thematic element, regardless of the religious beliefs of the creators or audience.

Personal Reflection

You may choose to invoke (as opposed to recite by rote) the Lord's Prayer as a personal ritual or as part of your meditation or mindfulness practice, even if you do not adhere to a specific religious tradition.

You may find comfort, guidance, or a sense of connection through its words.

CHAPTER TWELVE

KEYS TO MASTERING YOUR EARTHLY PERSONALITY

KEY # 1 – Master your personal power.
KEY # 2 – Master your self-love; then your impersonal love.
KEY # 3 – Master your Wisdom.

Recap:
Your Earthly Personality

Self-actualising your Earthly Personality is the foundation stone for Earthly Living. Increasingly, people are becoming psychologically self-actualised but not necessarily spiritually self-actualised which is where we are heading. However, the foundations must always be laid first. Here are the signs of earthly success:

- Success in your field; making a positive difference in the world.
- Developed intellectual and emotional intelligence.
- Taking care of your physical/etheric body.

- Understanding of your personality structures and harmonising them
- Your modus operandi is finely honed.

Holistic Health

Over decades of dedicated study into the teachings of spiritual masters, delving into metaphysics, and exploring the depths of spiritual psychology, alongside recent advancements in light and resonance technologies, a consensus has emerged: the Living Light of Divinity and the integration of our divine essence are integral to nurturing the body's innate ability for homeostasis and self-healing.

It is widely believed that without acknowledging these spiritual dimensions, humans who are solely fixated on material pursuits, can only access a fraction of our inherent capacity for self-renewal. Some estimations suggest this fraction may reach up to 30% in optimal circumstances. This perspective gains significance when one surveys the current state of individuals and the planet at large, witnessing widespread disharmony and disconnection that obstruct the realisation of optimal health.

The prevalence of energy blocks and negative influences further underscores the urgency of addressing these spiritual aspects. This urgency serves as the underlying motivation for the exploration presented in this book. While this perspective may not be readily validated within the empirical volumes of conventional science, it resonates profoundly within spiritual and holistic traditions. These traditions offer invaluable insights into the interconnectedness of mind, body, and spirit in the pursuit of well-being and wholeness.

By embracing and integrating these spiritual dimensions, we embark on a journey towards holistic healing – one that acknowledges the intricate dance between the physical, mental, emotional, and spiritual aspects of our being. It is through this synthesis that we pave the way for true transformation and the realisation of our fullest potential.

Individual Integration

Your Soul is the intermediary between your earthly personality and the Monad or Spirit of Divinity called Heaven; also called 'Higher Self or God-self.' Personality, Soul, and Monad make up the Threefold Constitution of man. Once harmonised holistic health is attainable.

Global Integration

On the universal scale, Humanity, Shamballa, and the Hierarchy make up the Threefold Constitution of earthlings' collective Divinity. Once harmonised global holistic health becomes attainable.

BEAUTY THERAPY FOR THE SOUL

One of the mottos I recall from my earlier career as a beauty therapist outlines a skincare routine, which I now use as an analogy for the evolution of consciousness across the three dimensions of earthly living – physical, mental/emotional, and spiritual. Just as this routine is vital for maintaining healthy skin, it proves equally crucial for the development of the soul, transcending subjective truths.

Beauty Therapy for the Soul forms the foundation of both my work and this book. Indeed, its influence extends to encompass the environment and all systems when viewed from a broader perspective. Below are a few ideas on which you can expand.

ASTRAL

CLEANSE – TONE – NOURISH – PROTECT
'Simultaneous Self-Harmonising 101'

The Cleanse
Cleanliness is next to Godliness

Physical:
1. Hydrate with pure (or blessed) water.
2. Practice regular detox routines.
3. Clean up your habits and behaviours.
4. Clean and declutter your home, garden, vehicles, and workspace.
5. Tidy up your records.
6. Eliminate grime and toxins within and without.
7. Keep your physical body clean.

Mental/Emotional:
1. Clean up your communications – inner and outer.
2. Practice self-reflection and let go of limiting beliefs.
3. Transcend negative thoughts and emotions including judgement.
4. Practice self-forgiveness and forgiveness of others.
5. Release mental clutter through meditation and relaxation.
6. Engage in physical activities that release mental tension.
7. Evaluate and clean up the company you keep, watch, and listen to.

Spiritual:
1. Engage in spiritual practices that help purify the mind, such as prayer, visualisations, or quiet meditation.
2. Seek spiritual guidance for clarity and peace.
3. Exercise self-love.
4. Exercise self-responsibility.

5. Exercise self-empowerment.
6. Engage in physical activities that bring spiritual clarity such as nature walks.
7. Say The Lord's Prayer with full consciousness of its meaning.

The Tone

Physical:
1. Exercise regularly for strength and flexibility.
2. Act on your dreams and affirmations.
3. Practice your physical skills, such as singing, dancing, teaching, painting, drawing, and communicating.
4. Beautify your surroundings.
5. Seek new friends with similar values.
6. Connect physical exercise with mental and emotional well-being.
7. Behave and act consciously.

Mental/Emotional:
1. Cultivate mental resilience through positive affirmations and cognitive exercises such as self-hypnosis.
2. Identify your highest values and virtues and live them.
3. Read, watch, or listen to uplifting teachings and music.
4. Act upon new skills such as standing in your power.
5. Develop mental strength and emotional intelligence through challenges, problem-solving and a focus on positive outcomes.
6. Practice self-love and self-nurturing.
7. Practice giving and receiving.
8. Practice 'Grace over Drama' consistently.

Spiritual:
1. Practice rituals or exercises that strengthen your spiritual connection.

2. Breathe self-love in long full breaths.
3. Enlist assistance from your Guardian Angels.
4. Practice detachment from negative energies.
5. Live to your highest values.
6. Practice non-judgment of self and others.
7. Practice harmlessness and compassion.

The Nourish

Physical:
1. Maintain a balanced diet with wholesome, nutrient-rich foods.
2. Include brain-boosting foods.
3. Breath self-love consistently.
4. Eat in alignment with your spiritual values.
5. Have a massage – nurture yourself.
6. Beautify your surroundings.
7. Be present in the moment with all activities.

Mental/Emotional:
1. Feed your mind with knowledge and positive influences.
2. Consume positive content.
3. Nurture and set boundaries for your inner child.
4. Nurture more supportive relationships.
5. Surround yourself with supportive friends with similar values.
6. Celebrate your inner beauty.
7. Nourish and grow your wisdom.

Spiritual:
1. Nourish your soul through spiritual literature, teachings, and practices.
2. Grow your wisdom.
3. Practice self-love and long full breathing.

4. Nourish your spiritual side for a balanced mind.
5. Have spiritual discussions with friend.
6. Practice connection with the spiritual hierarchy.
7. Listen to guided meditations such as I AM University ascension activation meditations.

The Protect

Physical:
1. Prioritise safety - use protective gear and products when needed.
2. Protect your intellectual and physical property, your computer, your car, and your savings.
3. Discern the company you keep.
4. Filter and bless your water.
5. Ensure a safe and comfortable environment.
6. Use more organic products on your body and in your environment.
7. Eat more organic food to support your physical wellness.

Mental/Emotional:
1. Establish healthy boundaries.
2. Practice detached involvement (neutrality) in relationships and discussions.
3. Practice discernment and stand in your power.
4. Practice self-responsibility with compassion and awareness.
5. Protect your mental well-being from negative influences.
6. Cultivate a positive mindset and embrace positive affirmations.
7. Shield your mind from negativity.

Spiritual
1. Surround yourself with positive energies.
2. Protect your spiritual space through meditation and superconscious energy practices.

3. Use God's Golden egg of Protection morning and night.
4. Protect your spiritual energy through grounding exercises and spiritual boundaries.
5. Release attachments.
6. Listen to guided spiritual protection meditations.
7. Listen to guided affirmation meditations or make your own.

Everything you imagine, think, and do, whether unconsciously or consciously, across all realms, interacts with every dimension of your being. Just as these aspects are interconnected within your energy system, they are also entwined with the entirety of existence.

Your vibrational influence carries a significant impact on the well-being of everyone and everything.

This implies that even the influence of those who are grossly unaware affects the entire collective. Thus, there is a necessity for protection from the dark emotions and thought forms that linger in the lower astral plane.

CHAPTER THIRTEEN

FORT KNOX AND THE GOLDEN EGG

Fort Knox is used here as a metaphoric highly secure depository for golden assets and precious items.

The metaphor of Fort Knox is often used to describe an exceptionally secure or impregnable place, symbolising a location or situation with high levels of protection, safety, or inaccessibility. In conversations, it conveys a sense of extreme security and safeguarding of valuable assets.

As you journey through the invisible realms of your soul, learn new techniques, and anchor more authenticity into your everyday life, it is important to guard what you have learned and prevent it from being sullied by negative energies, whether your own knee jerk reactions or from some of the other sources we have been alluding to:

ASTRAL

Energy Protection – Why?

*Unconscious aspects are always at play
every hour of the night and every hour of the day.
Your unconscious mind never ever rests.
It listens, it sees, it senses, it smells,
it hears, it tastes, it feels and digests.*

*As you carry on working or sleeping or talking
or sitting and gawking and listening and judging
and cooking and meeting and driving and eating...
it is ingesting, digesting, and under attack
by all kinds of things that will hack and hack!*

*Your unconsciousness mind is like a big sponge
absorbing all stuff from joy to grunge.
Much of it too is so unclear.
When you do know though - You are aware.
But it doesn't stop there ...*

If you are watching the news or a horror movie, say, in your state of 'trance' you will be absorbing willy-nilly all the trauma and emotions that are directed through the screen. How do you process it? Where does it go?

*Toxins are not just on the material plane;
There are invisible toxins that are more profane.
Not all is lost; there are things to do
To ensure you maintain the best of you.*

THE LAW OF FORTIFICATION
(Extracted from 'The Laws of the Light – Hidden Secrets Revealed by the I AM that I AM' by Ann Herbstreith)

"Fortify thyself with the All-Mighty Power available to you. Let no day go by except first you consciously surround yourself with this Mighty Energy. See it! Swirling clockwise and counter clockwise, a force so powerful that nothing can penetrate it. This is of the greatest importance in these times, for it shall become virtually impossible to keep out the race thoughts of negation and fear in any other way.

Protect yourself morning, noon, and night. Use this consciously; this is also important. You must be aware of this protection before it can become real to you. Only as you ask, can you receive. It is law.

This, then, is the law of fortification. Applying the Life Force of the universe to protect you against all negation, all disease, all things that are not for your highest good. This is your heritage, your gift of the Father. Before He sent you to earth, He knew the problems you would have to face – and would He send you unprotected? Oh, no! always this has been yours to use – but you have not remembered. Now the veil is being slowly drawn aside, and many things are being brought to remembrance. This mighty protection is yours to use, but, of course, it is still for you to use, or reject. So be it ever so."

ASTRAL

FORT KNOX OF THE SPIRIT

The 'Fort Knox' of the Spirit is a depository strong.
Where all is right and there is no wrong!
The currency of love can come and go,
And your highest virtues can flow to and fro.'

In courage and strength, the golden walls stand,
Supporting high values, as they contract and expand.
Wisdom and kindness, lending a hand,
Safeguarding your gateway to the 'Promised Land.'

A fortress so strong built with tender care,
Protecting your heart in a sanctuary rare.
The higher mind's treasures, all intertwine.
Sanctified energy in a radiant shrine.

Be aware and strive for this blessed place of Grace.
How precious it is to the human race!
For 'Heaven Above' is a state of mind.
Claim your inheritance now and don't lag behind.

Where the Love of all Love meets the Light of all Light
and the Wisdom of all Wisdom meets the Might of all Might
All energies harmonise in a synthesis of Grace.
The CREATOR OF ALL created this space.

It can only be accessed through the inner you.
Through the choices you make and the things that you do.
Clear all the energies blocked with fear.
And you will see clearly then, you're already THERE!

FORT KNOX AND THE GOLDEN EGG

Negativity and darkness must not get near.
They belong where the energy is thick with fear.
In the low astral plane- sullied by man,
Who is unaware of the Divine Mighty Plan.

To clear and protect your own energy,
Is as important for you as it is for me.
Protect your kids and colleagues too
from the dark emotions they are journeying through.

So fortify your personal space of grace,
With the virtues and gifts that you embrace.
Where the beauty of Love leaves its golden trace
Fort Knox for the Spirit is your Sacred Place!

GODS' GOLDEN EGG OF PROTECTION

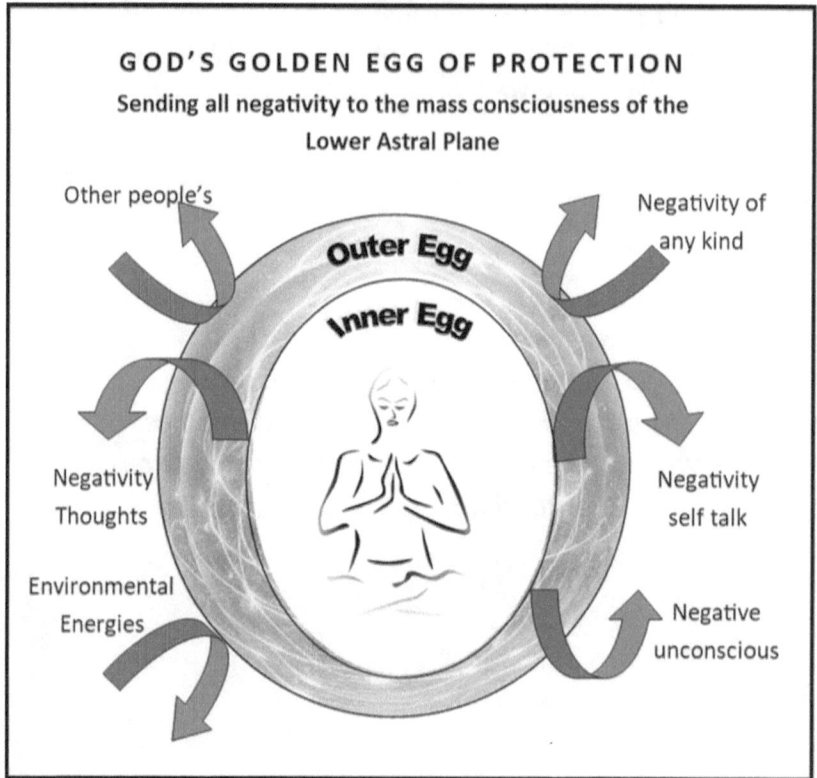

Visualisation

Close your eyes and envision a serene nature scene. Picture yourself smiling, radiating happiness, joy, love, and inner peace. Immerse yourself in the vibrant colours, fragrances, sounds, and the harmonious feeling of being one with nature. Observe butterflies gracefully fluttering, birds singing overhead, and feel a gentle breeze caressing you. The temperature is perfect, and the sun's rays warm your skin, reminding you of the inner light within.

Take a full breath in and exhale deeply. The air is pure, filled with the divine light and presence of God, a sacred experience as you breathe in the natural essence of divinity. As you walk on the grass, surrounded by mountains, lush greenery, and exquisite flowers, the deep blue sky promises miracles and wonders.

In this inner paradise, your God appears and envelops you in a swirling Golden Egg of Protection. This semi-permeable golden egg shields you from external negativity, blocking out adverse influences from people, events, and the world. Simultaneously, it wards off internal negativity — negative thoughts, feelings, temptations, bad habits — these bounce off the golden egg like a rubber pillow.

Visualise the golden egg as an impenetrable shield, permitting only goodness from the world and within yourself. Feel completely safe, protected, and invulnerable on all levels of your being. You embody the Realised Christ within the swirling Golden Egg of God's love, wisdom, and power.

Express gratitude to God for this gift, walk through the grass, and gently return to your everyday world. When you are ready, open your eyes.

GOD CONSCIOUSNESS

Consciousness is direct knowing, transcending belief and existing beyond any doubt. It permeates every electron and proton, swirling in an undefined form at an exact speed without direction. Consciousness is eternal – now, forever, and always, embodying Life itself. Imagine a vastness beyond human comprehension, filled with Life, known as 'energy,' in scientific terms. While scientists comprehend planetary formations based on electrons, protons, and gases, they often overlook the Intelligence or Consciousness within and behind everything.

This Intelligence, referred to as God in the world, is a name that fails to convey a true understanding, suggesting a separation between the Creator and His creation. The world's prayers to a distant 'God' perpetuate an illusory state of thinking. In ancient times, some sought power over others, deeming the idea of an 'All Powerful Oneness' sacrilege. This illusion served its purpose, as humanity struggled to grasp the essential truth. Man looked outward to a Power beyond himself, yet this power is within, waiting to be acknowledged and utilised. Mere knowledge is insufficient; one must, as volumes of Sacred Law including the Bible instruct, *"Prove me now"* in one's own life and affairs.

Without consciousness, life would not exist. Jesus Christ's declaration, *"I am the Life,"* signifies an identification with all, understanding himself as the embodiment of all life. Grasping this truth fully is challenging, but when the world collectively comprehends it, peace will reign. Strife cannot persist between individuals, nations, or neighbours when this truth is acknowledged – as destroying another is akin to harming oneself.

THE ALL'S COMMON THREAD

Religions: While diverse in their practices and beliefs, <u>various religions share a common thread of offering prayers</u>, supplications, or invocations to the divine. Islam has Al-Fatiha, Judaism has the Shema, Hinduism has the Gayatri Mantra, Buddhism has the Metta Sutta, Sikhism has Ardas, and Christianity, in addition to the Lord's Prayer, has the Hail Mary and the glorification of the Sacred Trinity. Despite differences in rituals and theological concepts, these prayers express a universal human longing for guidance, compassion, and connection with a higher power.

Indigenous and Tribal Spiritual beliefs often embrace a profound sense of oneness, emphasising the interconnectedness of all living beings and the natural world. For instance, within these traditions, the concept of oneness extends beyond human boundaries to encompass animals, plants, and the entire ecosystem. The natural world is revered as sacred, embodying a divine presence, and spiritual energy is perceived in everything, from rocks to trees.

Ancestral connections are considered part of this spiritual fabric, and ceremonies and rituals are performed to maintain harmony and balance, reinforcing the interconnected unity of individuals with their communities and the larger cosmic order. These diverse beliefs collectively reflect a holistic worldview that celebrates the spiritual oneness of all existence.

The concept of oneness or connection with the divine extends beyond individual beliefs, encompassing mystical experiences, non-dual philosophies, and the idea of a universal consciousness. Symbols such as mandalas represent the interconnectedness of all things, and the notion of cosmic harmony suggests a grand, unified order in the cosmos.

Love and compassion are often seen as unifying forces, reflecting a divine essence present in diverse spiritual teachings. Additionally, ecological spirituality highlights the interconnectedness of all life, promoting environmental responsibility as a means of expressing oneness with the Earth. Embracing various dimensions, cultures, and perspectives, the understanding of oneness or God is deeply personal, shaped by diverse cultural, religious, and philosophical contexts across the globe.

Recognising the profound interconnectedness and spiritual dimensions present in various belief systems underscores the

<u>importance of integrating earthly and spiritual psychology</u>. By bridging these realms, individuals can cultivate a holistic understanding of their existence, acknowledging the spiritual essence within themselves and the interconnected web of all life.

This integration invites a conscious awareness of love, compassion, and environmental responsibility as essential components of both personal and collective well-being. As people navigate the intricate tapestry of their beliefs, a harmonious synthesis of earthly and spiritual psychology can foster a balanced, enriched perspective that contributes to personal growth, community cohesion, and a sustainable relationship with the broader cosmos.

It is important to note that while these religions may use different names and forms to address the divine, the underlying essence often reflects a shared understanding of a transcendent, singular force that unites humanity in its spiritual quest.

CHAPTER FOURTEEN

BUSTING THE KARMA DRAMA

Karma serves as a path for spiritual evolution, guiding the soul's growth. In contrast, sin is an expression of ego rather than a spiritual concept."

*To Evolve your Soul and bring Heaven to Earth
is the Cause and Effect of Birth after Birth.
To break your Karma is the Effect of the Cause,
To be born and to die, under all types of Laws.*

*Hundreds of lifetimes, you'd think that we'd know.
Hundreds of deaths, where do we go?
Be willing to change with forgiveness too.
For Life is eternal it really is true.*

*Harmless and merciful to all who have erred.
These are the aims that have hardly been heard.
For not one of us, can cast the first stone.
NOW is the time for ALL to atone.*

By knowing yourself as much as you can,
Knowledge becomes wisdom; to grow the Great Plan.
Then Love above all and empowerment too.
Are beautiful virtues that will shine through you.

Simply put, 'Karma' is where the intent and actions of a person or group (the cause) influence the future of that individual or group (the effect). Good intent and good deeds contribute to good karma and happier rebirths for self and others, while destructive intent and destructive deeds contribute to bad karma and more challenging reincarnations for self and others.

BUSTING BAD KARMA
What a Palaver!

Obsession, Depression, Past Life Regression
Psychosis, Neurosis, Stress and Hypnosis.
On patterns and fears; we can all fixate.
Your choices and mine will seal our Fate.

What is Bad Karma?
Nothing but DRAMA!

A mesh of mistakes over eons of time
Some of them not even yours or mine.
Mistakes of ancestry all down the line,
Recycling the duality of EGO and time.

BACK IN TOUCH WITH PURPOSE AND KARMA

As mentioned earlier, you and I have lived many lifetimes full of challenges and opportunities to graduate from this School of Earth;

so, we can return to our essence and be free from the cycle of karmic re-incarnation. There is a higher purpose in the Great Divine Plan and each one of us has a part to play. Finding your particular and unique puzzle-piece can be challenging.

First, your individual initial responsibility is to harmonise your own earthly vehicle (your physical body) and your earthly concerns, like making a living, raising a family, developing friends, living a healthy toxic-free life (as much as possible), exercising, honing your skills, growing your knowledge, discovering your talents... recognising your passions, and so forth.

That is every human being's No. 1 purpose.

Simultaneously, as you grow your knowledge and conscious awareness, you can use your free will more wisely and powerfully. You can begin to develop and synthesise the higher multi-dimensional divine qualities of your mental, emotional, and spiritual bodies.

That is every human being's No. 2 purpose and what this book is about.

As that process unfolds, you will begin to recognise what amazing and unique skills you have, what 'floats your boat,' what it is you love to do, what you are passionate about, and the best thing is 'only you can do it' in the whole wide world.

The invisible laws that will be explored further will clarify the reasons why you go through the challenges you do; what happens when you do not meet them and more importantly what glorious events occur when you do.

THREE LEVELS OF KARMA

There are no judgements; but there is awareness!
Make a note of where you see yourself currently
on the Karma scale.

1. **Good Karma**
   In the process of <u>evolution,</u> you spiral your consciousness into the higher dimensions of yourself and anchor those virtues into life on Earth. You take command of your own destiny.
2. **Sad Karma**
   Traditionally the <u>status quo</u> is the process of revolution (going round in circles creating deeper and muddier ruts in life).
3. **Bad Karma**
   More destructive than sad karma is the process of <u>devolution</u> which is the descent to a lower or worse state of revolutionary degeneration.

Evolution? Revolution? Devolution? – Your Power of Choice!

SIN

Sin is an egotistical concept not a spiritual one.
It stems from a belief that mistakes become
indelible blemishes on your character.
We can forgive and be forgiven for our mistakes.
Forgiveness of self and others is the gateway to freedom.

Sad and Bad Karma (endarkened thoughts, ideas, images, and commands, frequently come from an unconscious sense of powerlessness, lovelessness, grief, shame, vengeance, despair, the need to be 'right' – the whole gamut; plus, the sins (mistakes) that we have inherited in our genetic makeup both through our forefathers and our past lives… <u>and our connection to mass consciousness</u> (The Astral Plane)!

Your astral body is either attentive to the egoic impression or swayed by the million voices of Earth. It has no voice of its own, no character of its own. The astral plane is the battleground of the soul, the place of victory or the place of defeat. Hence the need to master your thoughts, emotions, and choices wisely.

EVOLVING YOUR WISDOM

1. **Unconscious Incompetence**: Always be aware that there's more to know and more to explore. Before encountering added information or experiences, you might not be aware of what you lack knowledge about. This reflects a state of '<u>unconscious incompetence</u>,' where you don't know you don't know something; or you don't recognise your deficiencies.

2. **Conscious Incompetence**: As you learn and gain new insights, you become aware of what you didn't know previously. This marks a transition to '<u>conscious incompetence</u>,' where you realise your lack of knowledge in certain areas. It can be a humbling experience when you become aware of how much you need to learn or develop. Acknowledging that there is always more to learn fosters humility and an openness to continuous growth. No matter how much you learn, there will always be new discoveries and areas of ignorance to confront.

3. **Conscious Competence**: When you acquire the necessary skills and knowledge through practice and learning you transition into '<u>conscious competence</u>.' However, using those skills still

requires your conscious effort and focus. You know what you know, but you need to concentrate on applying that knowledge and skill effectively.

4. **Unconscious Competence:** When you have mastered a skill or knowledge to the point where it becomes second nature you have become 'unconsciously competent.' You can perform a task or demonstrate knowledge effortlessly and without consciously thinking about it. It has become ingrained in your subconscious, and you can operate with competence on an automatic level.

As you make progress through the stages above in your own life, you will undoubtedly recognise your learning and skill development follows an exponential growth curve, where the rate of improvement accelerates significantly once you move from conscious incompetence to conscious competence. However, if you are unconsciously competent in an area and are then required to teach it from scratch, you would need to revisit your consciously competent state – such as, (Heaven forbid!) if I ever needed to teach someone to drive.

These steps serve as a reminder that learning is an ongoing and never-ending process. The more you learn, the more you come to understand the vastness of human knowledge and the complexity of the world around you. It encourages a humble and curious mindset, where you are willing to explore innovative ideas and remain open to an ever-expanding realm of knowledge which is then available to use wisely and with discernment.

Always keep in mind that you, your colleagues, family, peers; the entire population of the Planet, are unique and at different stages of the karmic journey. Respect, forgiveness, compassion, harmlessness and non-judgement of self and others are vital practices; primarily, within your own being and then in service to others.

The axiom 'you don't know what you don't know, until you know' has been widely used and disseminated over time, it has become part of the collective wisdom shared in various educational, philosophical, and self-improvement contexts.

THE ATTRACTOR FACTOR
PHYSICAL, MENTAL, EMOTIONAL, SPIRITUAL

Swiss psychiatrist, Carl Jung taught:
*"What you resist persists.
It not only persists, but it will grow in size."*

What he meant by that is the more you resist anything in life, the more you bring it to you. The reason you attract whatever you resist is because you are powerfully focused on it with strong feelings and emotions, and what you focus on with any emotion, you bring to you. Hence the encouragement to always focus on an <u>ideal outcome</u>. You can use it to your advantage.

ASK AND YOU SHALL RECEIVE
MAKING IT REAL IS YOUR RESPONSIBILITY

There exist many Spiritual beings with specialties, some having lived on Earth and others not. It is never too late to seek help from cosmic spiritual beings and masters dedicated to the Divine Master Plan, of which we are all a part. The psychology of the spirit revolves around expanding consciousness, love, power, and wisdom in a balanced and synchronised manner on all dimensions of your Being.

These Divine Beings are all part of the multi-dimensional 'Oneness' or the 'Great I AM that I AM' expressing through you.

THREE LINES OF SPIRITUAL EVOLUTION

1. **The Elohim** are <u>creative</u> thought attributes of God.
2. **The Archangels and Angels** are <u>feeling</u> tones of God.
3. **The Ascended Masters** are the <u>balance</u> between the two.

These enlightened beings are radiant manifestations of light intricately connected to you through the divine matrix of the ALL, where both you and I find our distinct expression. They personify unconditional love, wisdom, and power, showcasing an expansive array of gifts, abilities, and intellects that surpass conventional belief. These entities have adeptly cultivated their higher cosmic light bodies and wholeheartedly contribute to the Divine Plan across multiple dimensions.

While a few Ascended Masters who have transcended their ego reside on Earth, the majority exist in spiritual form. Some are extra-terrestrial entities actively safeguarding Earth, while others serve as educators, imparting higher knowledge to those formulating plans for elevated service to the Divine Plan.

It does no harm to invoke Archangel Michael to envelop you in God's Golden Egg of Protection before attempting to connect with the Hierarchy. This ensures that, prior to invoking any light beings, you are in a state of grace and have sought protection, as there are deceptive entities on the lower astral plane that may exploit the vulnerable or unaware.

Guardian Angels:

While initially planned for later in the book, addressing this topic now seems timely. As a Spiritual Being undergoing an earthly experience, it's vital to recognise that many in your spiritual family have shared previous lifetimes with you but may not presently be incarnated on Earth. Some of these souls have ascended to higher states of being and willingly act as your guardians or guides, watching over you.

Every soul is assigned at least two guardian angels to assist in the evolutionary journey on earth. While you may be aware of their presence, many individuals are unaware that these angels are constantly by their side. A Spiritual Law prohibits direct assistance unless explicitly asked, but they can intervene in life-or-death situations – an insight for me gained through many firsthand experiences.

Communication with your personal angels is easily facilitated, and the process is private, as they intimately know you and can perceive your thoughts. The familiar adage, *"Why worry when you can pray?"* reflects the acknowledgment that prayer isn't a plea but rather a request for assistance during challenging times. To benefit fully, you must be receptive.

For example, (why not try it now?), take a breath and quietly ask your guardian angels for a sign of their presence or request a love wash. Then, in stillness, allow the experience to unfold. The manifestation varies from person to person –I feel warmth and love in my heart and throughout my body, while others may sense tingling, hear sounds, receive messages, see colours, or simply feel a sense of wellbeing. Each unique experience is right for the individual.

Similar to self-realisation, prayer, and angel realisation surpass mere belief; they establish a connection with the matrix of Life within the inner dimensions of your Beingness.

Specialty Angels:

Various angels specialise in addressing specific issues. For example, angels resonating with a platinum frequency can be invoked for healing purposes in any body part. Among the **Archangels** only two – Metatron and his brother Sandalphon – have lived and experienced life on Earth.

This vast topic has been extensively covered in numerous books and documented channellings, some of which are listed in the appendix at the end of this book. It's not necessary to have exhaustive knowledge about angels, archangels, and ascended masters to seek their assistance. However, it is always advisable to do some research on their specialties to grow your knowledge and wisdom.

Omnipresent Beings:

There are many who can be everywhere at once, such as Mother/Father God, the Christ, the Holy Spirit, and Archangel Michael, who holds leadership roles among archangels and oversees the life purpose of lightworkers. Archangel Michael's primary function is to eliminate the toxins associated with fear on Earth, wielding his renowned flaming blue sword, which among other skills can be used through the power of your imagination and request to cut attachments to drama. Archangel or Lord Michael is a very useful archangel to have on your team.

I can call on the God Force when I'm in a bind.
The prayers are always answered I find.
I breathe deeply and let the energy flow.
Beautiful colours that make drama go.

I come up with new choices to move ahead.
I practice forgiveness each night in my bed.
I cut my attachments to all the drama.
I thank the Creator who transmutes the bad karma.
I call for an anchoring of the goodness within.
Then, God's egg of gold light I spin, and I spin.
All around and about, within and without.
An Egg of protection that keeps negativity out.
And allows nothing but LOVE's energy without a doubt.

SPIRITUAL LEADERSHIP

In the realm of Spiritual Psychology, the journey involves not only expanding your light and aura but also embracing Spiritual leadership, service work, and a broader sense of citizenship. While individuals focus on their personal realisation, they concurrently aspire to elevate their consciousness to much higher levels. For instance, someone dedicated to global citizenship may simultaneously hold within their consciousness ideals of solar, galactic, universal, multi-universe, and cosmic citizenship.

This multidimensional perspective applies to various aspects mentioned earlier. Spiritual psychology emphasises the simultaneous existence and work on multiple dimensions. The ideal in Spiritual psychology is to embody light through realisation. The ongoing effort is akin to polishing a diamond, aiming to eliminate all blemishes, dark spots, or grey areas.

The concept of evolution is visualised as a spiral, where individuals continually navigate through the same lessons and Spiritual tests, albeit at progressively higher levels along the spiral. In this way, the journey is a dynamic process of growth and refinement, advancing towards greater spiritual understanding and enlightenment.

MESSAGES FROM THE MASTERS

THE COLOUR SPIRAL

From St Germain:
You live in swirling colour, (for vibration is also colour) but you do not see this, only at rare intervals. Now, as your thoughts spiral upwards, (and indeed it is only your thoughts or consciousness that spirals) you raise your vibration, or colour. The higher the thought the finer the vibration, the deeper the colour.

Now at a low rate of vibration the colour is a dense greyish essence, taking on hues of light blue, green, lavender, and pink. Intense emotion changes the colour, or vibration, therefore in moments of great love the colour takes on a deep rose, and vibration into a red, the highest.

Anger, or the negative emotion takes on the dark black, or densest colour.

Compassion vibrates to purple, the greater the compassion, the deeper the colour. When you sit in meditation, your thoughts spiral upward and if you are blessed you spiral into all Light, or the golden essence of the Sun, or Life Energy.

Each centre within humankind vibrates to a distinct colour, therefore the healing machines, given a person in the objective, to be brought into being, shall heal with colour therapy – i.e., if a person comes with a faulty heart, the machine shall beam upon them the blue ray. ** If the liver is affected, the green ray shall heal that. Now if a person shall treat their centres with colour each day – they shall literally be a God among humans, for first and foremost the admonition is: heal thyself. The higher the consciousness that person attains to, the deeper the tone of their vibration, for they then become the same essence of the Father which is Pure Spirit.

When speaking the Word for healing it is necessary to put force or power behind it, for the vibration, or colour behind the Word of authority is of a deep colour and must accomplish that which it is sent out to do. A weak command is lost in the aura of the one sending it and is not effective.

So now you have colour therapy. Use it to heal thyself; send it out when asked and share this wisdom with all whom you know shall understand.

Note: St Germain refers to future Light and Colour Technology that can help healing. Decades later, this has come to pass. I have included details of this technology in the appendix. I utilise this and other technology in my clinic to support holistic health and the messages within this book.

DAILY EXERCISE

Upon rising stand or sit quietly – visualise the Christ Blue entering the top of your head – filling full each atom of your being. Give thanks. Then visualise the purple flame filling your aura. This is the cleansing. Now visualise this purple turning into a soft rose colour. This fills your aura with the Love essence. When you feel this has penetrated your being visualise it going out from you to touch all living things on earth, and yet beyond.

Now visualise the bright green. Just literally bathe in it. It brings a sense of <u>well- being</u> – it acts upon your abundant life or brings into your life – all good – for no life is full and complete where there is lack of any good thing needed.

When you are weary – stretch up your arms overhead – your fingers spread and ask for the golden essence of the Sun to fill your being. This is the <u>Power of God</u>, or the Life essence, and does <u>restore, or give energy</u> but you must know this.

For <u>quick energy</u> visualise a flash of cherry red. In moments of pondering, or reasoning, see your brain centre bathed in yellow. All learned men of olden times wore yellow for it <u>works on brain cells</u>.

It is important when <u>sending healing</u> to send the Great White Light, for in this is contained all colours. The one receiving the White shall appropriate that which is more needed.

Many have come to the 'doorway,' only to turn back. That is as it should be, for as long as humans have a mission to perform on earth, they shall keep their feet on the ground but having changed their vibration – or transmuted even momentarily, they shall not be the same again, for once tasting life they cannot be satisfied with the 'husks.' Their one desire, then, becomes a need to help all struggling humanity, and to this end do they walk the earth. There can be no other purpose but to serve – Life – or ME! I AM St Germain.

Why worry when you can pray?

When you are in a hole, what choices have you got?
Climb right out or stay there and rot!

CHOICE IN THE NOW MOMENT

Every moment in time, you have choice. That is your power. Whichever way you choose, you are responsible for the consequences of your choices. Out of the apparent chaos of these times, each soul can make personal powerful and vital life changes that will also affect humanity and the planet either for better or for worse. <u>RIGHT NOW</u>, every individual on the Planet is faced with the choice of one of two options; and there are only two. It's as simple as that!

RIGHT NOW, is the only time you can be.
As you read on further you will hopefully see
Your past is past, 'though in memory it stays.
'til <u>forgiveness</u> transmutes your sad yesterdays!

The future is yours; it already exists.
Step into the mould that fits and assists,
Sense it and feel it without delay.
For your future is now, there is no other way.

In the vertical world you're a Living Light Being
In your physical body that takes some foreseeing.
Seasons and tides and calendar days
Record linear time in all sorts of ways.

But you can't measure time; the moment is NOW.
And the now is now, no matter how
You look at the moment, the moment is here.
There is no other moment but now, anywhere.

Choice #1

To rediscover (within the vertical dimensions) the fresh clean Utopia within your own consciousness where already resides the Living Light of All joy, health, harmony, forgiveness, love, power, wisdom, compassion, creativity, sharing, gratitude, unlimited abundance, eternal bliss... (and so on).

When Sai Baba defined 'God equals man minus ego" (meaning the negative ego), he also meant that underneath all the negative stuff and subjective beliefs, you are a unique expression of God, the Intelligence that is your Father/Mother Creator.

Note: In making Choice #1 there is no room for negative ego, none whatsoever! That means no judgements, no unforgiveness, no vengeful thoughts, no powerlessness, no victimhood, no irresponsibility. You and I deserve better than those dirty shades of grey that cause destruction and disease. In choosing Choice #1, you are on the high road to becoming the true expression of your highest consciousness, your Monad, or God-self. You embody forgiveness, love, blessings, power, responsibility, and wisdom.

Benefits: You get to embody and feel on every level of your being, all the ideal qualities of your Divine birth right. And you get to make a positive and authentic difference within your sphere of influence and within mass consciousness. You will experience your own authenticity. Your world becomes more joyful as you live your highest virtues, your awareness spirals upward and you embody and integrate the highest qualities in your daily life. You enhance the dynamics of relationships.

Choice #2

To re-create the same old, outdated journey of destruction of linear history (horizontal timeline) founded on traditional egoic teachings and skewed patterns of thoughts; based on fear, ingrained egoic beliefs and <u>relative or subjective truths</u>.

<u>Note</u>: In making Choice #2, you at least exercise your <u>power of choice</u>. However, you will not be using the other two vital ingredients of Divine <u>wisdom</u> (enlightenment) and eternal <u>love</u>. You get to keep on doing the same thing; you will end up where you are headed - Same as! The domino effect but with renewed awareness. Be aware now, with heightened awareness comes new responsibility.

Benefits: You exercised your <u>power of choice</u>. You raised your awareness of your own power. You know you do not need to be a victim of circumstances outside of you. By choosing to carry on reading this book, your awareness may be raised more. You will more thoroughly understand you are responsible for any consequences on your own inner wellbeing. i.e., without the other two ingredients of wisdom and self-love, you may not experience the beautiful gifts hidden within every challenge.

You will be reincarnated at the same consciousness stage you left this Planet. You will have another chance to go through those challenges/lessons you chose not to transmute or transcend, all over again in your next incarnation. You will pick up where you left off albeit in a different physical body and different circumstances.

Sitting on the Fence

In not making a choice at all you get to keep on doing the same thing; you remain a victim to circumstances and will end up where you are headed – a state of devolution. The downward domino effect.

<u>Benefits</u>: Your Egoic fear-based beliefs will take you to the end of your life 'dead right' in your subjective truth!

SEVEN QUESTIONS TO ASK YOURSELF WHEN MAKING ANY LIFE CHANGING DECISION

1. *Is it better to stay with the 'devil' I know? Or transcend the fear and try another tack?*

2. *Am I practicing compassion, forgiveness, and harmlessness in this choice?*

3. *What actions take me closer to Self and God-actualisation, to my passion, my unique puzzle piece; the very reason why I am here on Earth?*

4. *What beliefs and actions take me away from that purpose?*

5. *If I make this choice, where will it take me? Where will I be in 5 years or 10 years as the effect of this choice?*

6. *Am I choosing in love, wisdom, and power?*

7. *Where will I be if I make no choice at all?*

If you genuinely want inner peace, authenticity, and health, you will find your answers.

"<u>Willingness</u> is the driving force for transformation of any kind; <u>Imagination</u> is its playmate."
(J. Krishnamurti)

To you who are willing to follow your unique life purpose and evolve out of old stuck habits that no longer work, the Divine principles and secrets that are hidden within the dimensions and densities of your mind are where you will find your answers. You too have been the recipient of many signs and guidance in a variety of ways. Have a think about it.

What have you acted upon? What have you ignored? Have you used your power of choice? Or have you discarded your dreams of magnificence as unachievable and too hard to pursue?

The power of free choice, also known as free will, is your fundamental capacity to make decisions and choices that are not determined by external factors, fate, or predestined outcomes. It is the idea that you can act independently, based on your own thoughts, intuition, desires, and values.

Free will is God's gift to man
You make your choices because you can.
The autonomy to choose for better or worse,
Creations of goodness or quite the reverse.

Love over fear - the choice is yours
Better the cause of the effect,
than the effect of the cause.

Integration Example:

A Litte Gem adapted from the IAM University's Threefold Flame Chart of Power Love and Wisdom:

Power without Love creates Hitler mentality.

Power without Wisdom creates a path to hell paved with good intentions.

Love without Power creates women who love too much.

Love without Wisdom creates conditional and dependent love.

Wisdom without Power creates 'Ignorance is Bliss'.

Wisdom without Love creates 'intellectualism'.

Love, Wisdom, and Power create 'Integrated Ascended Masters' – that perfect balance between creative thought and feeling.

KEY ASPECTS OF CHOOSING TO LIVE YOUR LIFE IN LOVE, POWER, AND WISDOM

Autonomy: Choosing wisely with love and compassion grants you autonomy over your actions and decisions. It acknowledges that you are not merely a passive product of circumstance but have the power to shape your life positively.

Responsibility: The power of free choice comes with the responsibility to be informed and to take ownership of your decisions and their consequences. You and only you are accountable for the choices you make and the impact those choices have on yourself and others.

Morality and Ethics: Free choice raises important ethical considerations. It enables you to act according to your values, virtues, and moral principles, allowing you to make choices aligned with what you believe or discern is right or wrong.

Personal Growth and Development: The ability to make choices plays a crucial role in self-actualisation (personal growth) and development. You can learn from your choices, responses, and experiences, and adapt and evolve over time.

Intentional Decision Making: The power of free choice is associated with a holistic conscious decision involving options available, weighing consequences, and making deliberate choices based on the integration of reason, intuition, and higher love-based emotions.

DIVERSE OUTCOMES

Free choice allows for a wide range of possible outcomes and paths in life. It leads to the diversity of human experiences and contributes to the richness of human society. Utilising the power of free choice underpins many aspects of human life, including legal systems, personal responsibility, and the pursuit of individual happiness and fulfillment. It serves as a cornerstone of human identity and the basis for many societal norms and values.

You already know what I have chosen as a result of Trigger #111, but it has not always been so as you will find in the following pages. At times, the inner guidance I have personally resisted and ignored (traditionally labelled 'sins of omission' as opposed to 'sins of commission') have sometimes become so challenging for me I have been bought to the choice of either committing suicide or acting from my inner wisdom.

I have chosen wisely to live by Choice #1 and my voyage of discovery continues to spiral upwards.

You and I are similar in how we grow; however, every personality is on a stage of their evolutionary soul journey that is perfect for them right now. It really does not matter. What does matter is that you are conscious of that and give <u>respect</u> and educate yourself first and foremost. Why?

So, you can evolve a more authentic expression of your unique and authentic magnificence; and allow others to as well.

Then under <u>The Law of Correspondence</u>, you will <u>reflect that same respect</u> and authenticity into your outer environment. As you respect yourself, so will others respect you. As you become your more authentic self, so too will others be more authentic with you. As you become your more loving self, so will others be more loving towards you.

To hold compassion, forgiveness, and respect for all others no matter what they are struggling with, means you are instrumental in the health and wellbeing of humanity and the Planet. You are being of service not only to yourself, but also to your brothers and sisters.

THE CORRESPONDENCE OF THINGS

YOU ARE ME AND I AM YOU
We are all connected, it really is true.
ALL EXISTS IN THE DIMENSIONS OF YOU
And in all dimensions of everyone else too.

You may be unique in the way that you view,
But the way you express it must always be true.
There are no new ideas; no, nothing new,
Just ways of expression that keep coming through.

What is the message you express through you?
Is it distorted by ego, or pure and true?

UPWARDS and OUTWARDS and INTERNALLY
Consciousness Spirals through ETERNITY
Embodying Divine Virtues
Grounding them to Earth, is
THE SACRED PURPOSE OF HUMAN REBIRTH.

When AS ABOVE IS SO BELOW
And AS BELOW IS SO ABOVE
Pure Consciousness
Resonates IN LOVE.

Linear time is a myth don't you know?
It's there for earthlings to measure how they grow.
The time is NOW, the time is DUE,
To forgive all with mercy and compassion too.
For you are me and I am you!

ASTRAL

We are as cells in the great cosmos.
Part of the ALL reflecting our gloss
The light we emit, the way that we live.
The service, compassion, and inspiration we give.

The stem cell we are is one and the same.
Expressing the All, regardless of Name.

The tough Earth school challenges your resilience. Embracing choices, overcoming obstacles, and transcending challenges enriches your soul, aligning you with your authentic self through Spiritual Living Light Energy. The only exception is your negative ego, which should not be integrated.

Keeping in your enlightened unconditional love, power, and wisdom, your '<u>Sacred Trinity Space of Grace</u>' will automatically dissolve the negative ego's destructive effects on Life itself.

As mentioned previously, <u>the talents and passion you hold for your unique life purpose is a huge impetus for facing the challenges of life with grace and wisdom.</u>

The cause and effect of <u>a few</u> of the signs received during my own personal difficult times unfold further in this book. I see them as a journey of preparation, not for me to choose suicide, addiction, or a life of depression; but to turn my energies always to sharing and igniting in 'Divine Timing' an inspiration of those absolute truths and beautiful effects within you too.

Why?

Because we are all interconnected through the eternal energy of LOVE AND GRATITUDE. For when you begin to embody the gifts of your highest self, you will be eternally grateful. Love and Gratitude are the healing properties that the mana from Heaven (your LIFE Breath) will magnify within you. Love and gratitude have the power to create miracles both within and without.

It is the negative ego that blocks and destroys that connection of Oneness with ALL that is beautiful within and without; above and below. It is a lack of emotional intelligence or know-how that leads people to addictions, disease, and self-destruction.

You my beloved reader are unique in the way that you grow. Not everyone experiences their inner guidance as you or I do. Some recognise signs and patterns, some follow their intuition, some use kinesiology techniques, some have a gut feeling; some just know. Some consult their highest God-self, the Angelic Realms, and the Divine Hierarchy which, yes, live within the higher dimensions of your mind.

Others, of course, react automatically from the defensive position of Ego. It is the automatic kneejerk reactions, the resistance to, or the reliance on outside unwise advice that can cause chaotic effects in your own life and beyond.

Regard well what my words say,
But always go within to check your way.

For humans to have inner peace requires not only thinking and acting properly, but also learning to enjoy the peace that comes from no thought – or a peaceful quiet mind. There is a time to think and a time not to think – as in quiet meditation within the swirling golden light of God's Golden Egg of Protection.

CHAPTER FIFTEEN

PHYSICAL BRAINY STUFF!

WHY YOU MUST DETERMINE YOUR BEST OUTCOME

There is a system in your brain, the Reticular Activating System, that will filter your thoughts and notice your focus.

THE RETICULAR ACTIVATING SYSTEM (RAS)

The Reticular Activating System (RAS), located in the lower part of your posterior brain, plays a crucial role in sensory perception and attention. At any given moment, you are bombarded with sights, sounds, smells, tastes, and tactile inputs.

Consciously processing all this sensory information is impossible, so the RAS acts as a filter, selecting the stimuli to which you may consciously attend. Notably, signs in your external world often mirror the focus of your attention.

Yes, your environment reflects your thoughts!
Your energy flows where your attention goes!

Consider this: Imagine you have just acquired a brand-new *Ford Mustang* (if only) and the excitement is palpable. As you go about your daily routine, you begin to notice Mustangs on the streets, in magazines, in advertisements, and more – it's uncanny. Similarly, when you resist anything that you wish to avoid in your life, be it *"I don't want to be overweight," "I don't want to be impoverished,"* or even a simple reminder like *"I mustn't forget the milk when I go shopping,"* the RAS kicks in. What does it focus on? Weight; poverty; forget the milk!

THE AMYGDALA

After information passes through the RAS, it moves on to the amygdala. The amygdala then directs the information to either the lower reactive brain or the prefrontal cortex – the thinking brain – where you can reason out the received information. Notably, the prefrontal cortex doesn't fully mature until around 24 years old, offering insight into why some teenagers might not consider the consequences of their actions.

Now, consider moments of fear, stress, or anxiety, often triggered by automatic reactions to past experiences. The amygdala relays information to the reactive lower brain, initiating an automatic fight, flight, or freeze response. The adrenals spring into action; cortisol levels rise; happy hormones diminish. You may find yourself in a heightened state of vigilance, ready to confront the perceived threat, flee from it, or become immobilised.

This intricate physiological cascade, known as the stress response, represents a complex interplay between the brain and the body, preparing you to cope with various challenges. The dynamic interaction between the brain and the body not only illuminates your immediate responses but also underscores the importance of comprehending these processes in navigating the complexities of thoughts and emotions.

UNCONSCIOUS PATTERNS AND MENTAL HEALTH

These patterns can significantly influence your automatic emotional responses to similar situations in the present, even if you are not consciously aware of the underlying memories or associations.

In past trauma for instance, consider the case of a returned serviceman who has experienced combat deployment, enduring a constant fight-or-flight state of stress and emotions intensified by the sights and sounds of war and the continual flow of adrenaline. The physical and mental trauma brought back to the relative safety of home continues to be triggered by noises, smells, nightmares, and more. This example is similar to any trauma experienced throughout life; and there are too many to list, however, you my beloved reader will comprehend.

Trauma demands a thoughtful and compassionate approach, as it cannot be dismissed or alleviated through the numbing effects of alcohol, drugs, or detrimental behaviours. These misguided coping mechanisms often intensify the symptoms of anxiety, creating a vicious cycle of emotional distress.

The repercussions of trauma extend beyond the individual, affecting familial bonds and surfacing as stigmatising labels such as 'mental health issues.' Left unaddressed, these issues can gradually manifest as a spectrum of physical ailments, from common maladies like headaches and dizziness to more severe conditions such as panic attacks, strokes, diabetes, irritable bowel syndrome, obesity, and complex pain syndromes. Recognising the intricate connections between trauma and its diverse manifestations is crucial for fostering healing and promoting holistic well-being.

While this example is far from a simple matter of forgetting the milk, it vividly illustrates the compounding effects of certain causes. It emphasises the necessity to seek professional help when coping independently becomes challenging.

Engaging with the intricate dynamics of the amygdala and unravelling the unconscious patterns it retains opens up the possibility of processing and reframing past emotional experiences. This transformative process holds the potential to cultivate a more adaptive and constructive emotional response in the present.

The inclusion of Divine Intervention in this therapeutic journey can elevate the impact, introducing a profound dimension that transcends the conventional realms of psychological healing. The harmonious synergy between psychological exploration and spiritual intervention creates a holistic approach, fostering a deeper level of personal growth and emotional resilience.

CAUSE AND EFFECT OF CURRENT GLOBAL STRESS ON HEALTH SYSTEMS

A survey by the *Commonwealth Fund* suggests that approximately 75-90% of visits to primary care physicians are related to stress. It's crucial to emphasise that this estimation is not universally applicable and may differ from country to country. In the aftermath of the Covid-19 pandemic, primary care physicians have reported a notable surge in their workload. This surge has translated into an expanding workforce of stressed healthcare professionals managing an increasing number of patients experiencing heightened stress levels.

Whereas younger physicians (under age 55) were more likely to experience stress, emotional distress, or burnout; in nearly all countries, they were more likely to seek professional help compared to older physicians. Physicians who experienced stress, emotional distress, or burnout were also more likely to report they were providing a worse quality of care compared to before the pandemic.

In a remarkable display of self-awareness and dedication to their own well-being, some enlightened physicians have sought support for their stress by taking time out to visit me as an alternative healthcare worker who encourages the command of innate resources over the dispensing of medication.

These healthcare professionals, burdened with immense responsibilities for their patients (within the confined timeframe of a 10-20-minute consultation), grapple with a profound dilemma inherent in the Hippocratic Oath. Their commitment to the ethical principle 'to do no harm' clashes with the tangible weight of real-world responsibilities, where the outcomes of their services carry significant implications. This juxtaposition underscores the complex challenges faced by physicians who strive to balance their noble commitment to patient welfare with the intricacies and pressures of modern healthcare practice.

It is crucial to acknowledge that a significant portion, often half or more, of older physicians across various countries express their intention to cease patient care within the next three years. This trend paints a portrait of a primary care landscape increasingly dependent on younger, yet more stressed and burned-out physicians. In the present circumstances, a recognition emerges that 'something has to give.' By implementing radical and positive shifts in internal unconscious thought patterns and effectively managing stress as it arises, an enlightened vibration becomes a powerful factor contributing to global health.

THERE IS NO LOGIC WITH THE RAS AND THE AMYGDALA

These parts of your brain do not have the reasoning abilities to work out what is best for you. They simply respond back to your consciousness what they have been fed. They cannot reason out what the <u>implied effects</u> of why you <u>don't want</u> to be overweight, or poor, or diseased, or why you don't want to forget the milk.

The implied consequences are things you may unconsciously <u>fear might happen</u> if you do get overweight, are poverty stricken, continue to be diseased, or forget the milk. In other words, with the way you are asking, you may be compounding an effect that you don't want.

PROTESTING IS A POWERLESS ACTIVITY

Oh, the horrors! Those engaged in judgmental and vengeful discussions often remain oblivious to the fact that they are surrendering the power of their minds to someone else's endarkened thoughts and behaviours. Such groups, driven by a righteous stance against undesirable elements in their lives or the world, may even jeopardise their own well-being to make their point.

In such situations, it is more advisable to cultivate awareness of the issue or conspiracy and develop a practice of detached involvement when these matters arise. If necessary, taking a stand for the opposite or positive end of the spectrum is a more constructive approach. With your growing understanding of vibrational osmosis, the time may have come for you to make a choice.

If you find yourself part of such groups, you can either distance yourself or learn to maintain a detached involvement. Another option is to champion a cause that promotes a win-win outcome for all. Engaging in debates, arguments, or extreme actions like blocking traffic, akin to a child's tantrum of powerlessness, may not be the most effective way forward.

As Carl Jung wisely stated, *"What you resist persists."*

EXAMPLES OF THE RAS AT WORK

Now that you are conscious of how the brain responds with implied fear consequences, observe its operation in your own life. Consider how often you've uttered commonplace phrases with underlying warnings – such as reminding someone not to forget to clean their teeth, implying potential consequences if they do forget and the subsequent chain of fearful effects. Similar phrases like *'don't fall,' 'don't say a word,' 'don't drink and drive,' 'don't listen to social conspiracies,' 'don't bully,' 'don't be racist,' 'don't have a tantrum,' 'don't eat too much,' 'don't stay up all night on your device,' 'don't make such a racket,' 'don't argue,'* and *'don't be late'* are pervasive.

I've underlined what the brain tends to act upon. Take note of what persists, whose brain you're training, and whose power you're assuming. Ponder the implied consequences on families and communities. Consider the lasting impact over lifetimes. Awareness of these patterns prompts reflection on the subtle influence we exert on ourselves and others through such expressions.

Reflect on resistant thoughts that frequently occupy your mind or words you consistently say to yourself, such as 'don't <u>overreact</u>,' 'avoid that <u>second glass of wine</u>,' or 'refrain from <u>watching violent movies</u>.' These internal dialogues shape your mindset.

- Take note of what will persist.
- Observe whose brain you are influencing.
- Be aware of whose power you are assuming.
- Consider the implied consequences on your family and community.
- Ponder the potential implications over lifetimes.

Extend this analysis to the broader world and its systems. Examine the messages conveyed by leaders, social media, and the news, including the subtle blame and shame often directed at the public—whether consciously or unconsciously. Consider instances where fear is perpetuated:

In the political sphere: 'Expect a recession,' implying dire consequences if more taxes aren't collected from the public.

In environmental discourse: 'Worse weather and rising sea levels,' suggesting that without public action, the oceans will drown in plastic waste; neglecting to address broader issues like war pollution and corporate waste mismanagement.

In social campaigns: *'Stop Child Poverty,' 'Stop Child Abuse,' 'Stop smoking,' 'Stop drug trafficking,' 'Stop drink driving,'* and *'Stop crime.'*

In this context, the constant repetition of 'STOP' in various campaigns and messages may inadvertently reinforce the very issues these campaigns aim to address. The RAS, being non-discerning in terms of motive, may simply register the repeated negative terms, potentially reinforcing and amplifying the associated concerns in the individual and community consciousness.

Understanding the intricacies of how your brain processes information, especially through systems like the RAS, highlights the importance of choosing language and framing messages in a way that aligns with the desired outcomes and avoids unintentional reinforcement of negative patterns.

THE HUMAN - 'CYBER'MIND CORRELATIONSHIP

Metaphorically technology and the human mind draw parallels between the functioning of computer systems, particularly cyber networks, and the cognitive processes of the human brain. Here are some aspects of this metaphor:

Information Processing:

Tech - In cyber networks, information is transmitted, processed, and stored through interconnected nodes and pathways. Data is transferred at high speeds, enabling efficient information processing.

Human - Similarly, the human mind processes information through a vast network of neurons and synapses. When thoughts, memories, and sensory inputs are ideal the flow through the interconnected pathways is clear, allowing for efficient cognitive functions such as perception, memory, and decision-making.

Connectivity:

Tech - Nodes in a cyber network are connected, allowing for seamless communication and data exchange. The strength of a network lies in its ability to maintain connectivity and transfer information across various points.

Human - Similarly, neurons in the brain form intricate networks, enabling the transmission of electrical impulses and chemical signals. The connectivity of these neural networks is crucial for the seamless flow of information within the brain.

Parallel Processing:

Tech - Modern computer networks often employ parallel processing, where multiple tasks are executed simultaneously. This enhances efficiency and speed in handling complex operations.

Human - The human brain is capable of parallel processing, allowing it to handle multiple cognitive tasks simultaneously. This ability is evident in activities such as multitasking and simultaneous processing of sensory information.

Storage and Retrieval:

Tech - Cyber networks include storage systems where data is stored and can be retrieved as needed. The efficiency of data retrieval contributes to the overall functionality of the network.

Human - Human memories and information are stored in various regions of the brain. The brain's ability to retrieve stored information is crucial for tasks such as recalling facts, experiences, or learned skills.

PHYSICAL BRAINY STUFF!

Adaptability and Learning:

<u>Tech</u> - Advanced computer networks can adapt to changing conditions, optimising performance, and resource allocation. Machine learning algorithms enable systems to improve over time.

<u>Human</u> - The human brain exhibits <u>neuroplasticity</u>, allowing it to adapt to new experiences, learn from them, and form new neural connections. Learning and adaptation contribute to cognitive development and flexibility. That is what I am talking about!

Vulnerability to Malware:

<u>Tech</u> - Cyber networks are susceptible to malware and cyber threats that can compromise their integrity and functionality.

<u>Human</u> - Similarly, the human mind can be influenced by negative EGO thoughts, stress, or <u>external factors</u> that may impact mental well-being and cognitive functioning.

ARTIFICIAL INTELLIGENCE

Note: This paragraph was written solely by asking the free version of ChatGPT the following question: "Can you write me a paragraph on the human vulnerabilities of relying on Artificial Intelligence too much?"

Here is the unedited answer:

> "Relying extensively on artificial intelligence poses inherent human vulnerabilities that warrant careful consideration. As we integrate AI into various aspects of our lives, from

decision-making processes to critical tasks, there is a risk of diminished human agency and decision autonomy. Overdependence on AI may lead to an erosion of essential skills, such as critical thinking and problem-solving, as individuals may become accustomed to automated solutions. Moreover, there are concerns about privacy and data security, as increased reliance on AI involves the sharing of sensitive personal information. The potential for algorithmic bias also introduces the risk of perpetuating existing societal inequalities, as AI systems learn from historical data that may contain biases. Striking a balance between leveraging the benefits of AI and preserving human autonomy is crucial to navigating the complexities of an AI-driven future."

CYBER-SUMMARY

While the cyber metaphor highlights intriguing similarities between cyber networks and the human mind, it's essential to recognise the significant <u>differences in complexity, consciousness, and the qualitative aspects of the human condition that go far beyond the capabilities of artificial systems</u>.

The analogy draws a parallel between the maintenance needs of cyber networks and computer programs and the necessity for continuous mental upkeep in your human system. Just as cyber networks and computer programs benefit from regular defragging and updates to ensure optimal efficiency, your human mind also requires constant clean-up and refinement of mental and emotional programs for sustained well-being and optimum health.

Additionally, as personal computers have firewalls and anti-virus programmes, so too by the power of mental imagery and higher emotional vibration can you install protective processes for your own matrix of personal energy.

As I muse on this parallel to cyberspace
I appreciate the gift of human grace.
To own and employ the power of free choice.
Gives us so much more to voice and rejoice!

THE PHYSICAL BRAIN AND THE UNCONSCIOUS MIND

The brain and the unconscious mind are two distinct but interconnected aspects of human cognition and mental processes. Here's a brief differentiation between the two:

The Physical Brain:

The brain is a physical organ located within the skull and is a part of the central nervous system. It consists of different regions, including the cerebrum, cerebellum, and brainstem, each responsible for various functions.

The brain is involved in processing sensory information, controlling bodily functions, initiating voluntary movements, and supporting conscious awareness and cognition. It operates through electrochemical signals transmitted between neurons and synapses. It can be studied and understood through various scientific disciplines, such as neuroscience, anatomy, and physiology.

The Unconscious Mind:

The unconscious mind refers to a part of mental activity that operates beyond conscious awareness. It encompasses processes, thoughts, feelings, and memories that are not accessible to conscious awareness but can influence thoughts, emotions, and behaviours.

The unconscious mind is associated with automatic and involuntary processes, including instinctual drives, habits, and implicit learning. It is believed to store information, experiences, and memories that are not readily accessible to conscious recall.

The unconscious mind can influence behaviour, motivations, and perceptions, often manifesting through dreams, slips of the tongue, and various forms of symbolic communication. It is a concept often used in psychoanalysis, psychodynamic psychology, and other fields of psychology that focus on the exploration of the deeper layers of the mind.

While the brain is a physical organ that processes information and supports conscious awareness, the unconscious mind refers to the hidden aspects of mental activity that operate outside of conscious control. The brain provides the biological foundation for cognitive processes, while the unconscious mind encompasses psychological processes that occur beyond conscious awareness. Both play important roles in human functioning and are interconnected in shaping our thoughts, emotions, and behaviours.

CHAPTER SIXTEEN

SUPERPOWERS

Your superpowers they can't be seen,
'Though they influence your entire being.
When you're aware of them and know,
How to direct their powerful flow
You'll command them everywhere you go.

But do no harm I caution you here,
For any bad karma will adhere
And all the lessons you didn't learn,
Will be right here on your return.

So, make sure this time round,
To bring your Heaven to this ground.
Is this Earth better for hosting you?
Or will you have left some residue?

For the mistakes of lifetimes gone before
Forgive yourself I implore.
For your Karmic record will certainly show,
How well you did or didn't go.

HUMANITY'S GENERAL 'WILLY-NILLY' USE OF SUPERPOWERS

Despite the fact that the ageless wisdom of our innate superpowers and spiritual gifts of creation has not been widely disseminated to the majority of the world's population, these invisible powers persist, often operating haphazardly among the unaware. The manifestations crafted over lifetimes mirror humanity's ignorance of the inherent power residing within each individual, and the accompanying responsibility.

Unfortunately, some who have gained this awareness choose to keep this knowledge to themselves, primarily to exert power over others. Manipulating others, however, deviates from the ideal outlined in the Divine Plan of creation.

With awareness comes responsibility. Some would rather bury their heads in the sand and take no personal responsibility. I repeat the examples on the consequences of lack of integration given under the chapter on 'Karma Drama.'

Under the <u>Law of Correspondence</u>, our environment both within and without and further afield, reflects the effects of a huge percentage of the population's innate superpowers being used without education, discretion, direction, or protection. Look how a lack of education in ageless wisdom has affected our relationships with self and others.

Why are there so many people reaching for drugs, alcohol, and medications? Why are there so many addictions? Why is there a general lack of humility, and an unwillingness to forgive? Why are we so judgemental? Why do we need to be right? Why is there so much dis-ease and mental issues?

I could go on, but you get the drift.

What thoughts, images and words have we all imagined and uttered to take us away from the perfect Creation of ourselves? Where are they stored and what effect are they taking on our health, our systems, and the health of our planet?

THE INCREDIBLE POWER OF THE COLLECTIVE UNCONSCIOUS

From your exploration of the preceding chapters, you've gained insight into the potency of your unconscious mind, serving as the architect of your earthly experiences. Picture your unconscious mind as an iceberg, concealed 90% beneath the surface.

Now, contemplate the immensity of the collective unconscious — a conglomerate creation shaped by Earthly experiences, largely beyond any individual's conscious control. In the present global landscape, discussions around issues such as global warming, wars, and insurrections are manifestations echoing from this collective unconscious.

Existence unfolds across multiple planes, sub-planes, and degrees within the vast expanse of the ALL. The progression on these planes is intricately tied to the advancement of beings through specific scales of density. From the densest matter at the lowest point to the subtlest separation from the SPIRIT of THE ALL at the highest, there exists a continuous movement along this Scale of Life.

Every entity follows this path, with the ultimate destination being THE ALL. Despite appearances suggesting contradictions, the underlying truth is that all progress signifies a return home. The universal trajectory is one of perpetual ascent, irrespective of any seeming complexities. This, succinctly put, is the profound message of the enlightened.

ASTRAL CADASTRAL

Your thoughts are like radio waves in the air
You cannot see them, but they are there*.*

As you read through this book, we are taking a look
at where your thoughts and emotions go
And what they continue to do;
while they track their escape away from you.

For you not only have to deal
With what you think, believe, and feel.
You must be aware of those out there
Who have no scruples and do not care.

For they too have thoughts that roam
Where all thoughts go away from home
You see, you are not the only one
Struggling to thrive under this sun.

For aeons of time, you have been a sponge
Unconsciously hypnotised by too much grunge
The subjective beliefs of devil-may-care
Millions of people so unaware.
Dispensing negative ego everywhere.

Dark thoughts and feelings don't stick around
'Though I'd prefer them to 'go to ground'!

SUPERPOWERS

*The issue is - none of your thoughts remain
In the personal space of your immediate plane.*

*For while they're having their effect on you
They're also travelling eternally through
ALL other dimensions that are part of you too.*

**It's the higher planes where wise thoughts go
Where all is light, and love does flow
Where supportive energy runs to and fro'
And your Spirit travels there to grow.**

*But when thoughts are negative,
and your emotions are too,
They not only cause stress and illness for you
They blaze a trail away from you too.*

*They track a journey to the mass dark plane.
And in that lower astral they will remain.
They open a vortex from there to here
paving a road that lays you bare,
To other dark entities found out there.
(when you are unprotected and unaware)*

*The lower astral is a place so dire,
Where the collective dark ego plays with fire.
The state of all people comes down to the wire.
When we see the creations of such a quagmire.*

*It's urgently time to de-hypnotise
And clear the smut from your physical eyes.
For what you see may not be true
<u>Unless it echoes the Divine in you</u>.*

ASTRAL

WHAT DOES THE COLLECTIVE UNCONSCIOUS HAVE TO DO WITH GLOBAL WARMING?

Even the mineral, plant, and animal realms
Suffer at times from life's overwhelms.

When wind rages 'round, and rains pour down,
Drowning out your little town.
The seas surge and fires burn
And people's emotions are in a churn.

'Though the forces of nature may devastate,
It's part of the process, part of the plan
Affording the lessons, to WAKE UP MAN!

The vibrations and dimensions within the ALL
Can support ALL life or make it fall.
You have FREE WILL to make your choice,
To command your thoughts with an active voice.

To raise your vibration and play your part
Feeds the collective resonance of the Human Heart.
To use the Light of love given at birth.
Will help with the healing of Planet Earth.

HOLOGRAMS OF CONSCIOUSNESS

The concept of a 'holographic universe' is often explored in metaphysical and philosophical discussions, and in more recent times, scientifically. This idea suggests that the entirety of ALL that is, and aspects of it, can be likened to a hologram. The notion is inspired by the characteristics of holograms, where each part of the hologram contains information about the entire image.

SUPERPOWERS

We all have a responsibility to nurture ourselves and each other; such as in the metaphor of each one of us playing our instruments within the great orchestra of LIFE.

**The stem cell we are is one and the same.
Expressing the All, regardless of Name.**

You're a bundle of energy through and through
A hologram of consciousness
Is what makes you 'YOU.'
The awesome thing is ...
Holograms shape all else too!

Holograms are you.
Holograms are me.
Holograms are All.
You and I see.

Holograms of Heaven
Holograms of Hell?
Holograms for ill
Holograms for well?

What I see and what you see too
In your outside world,
Is a projection of you.

All bundles of energy correlate
When you master your own
You empower ALL fate.

Protect what you've learned
And be only concerned
With the goodness and love you can co-create.

THE POWER OF YOUR CONSCIOUS AND SUPERCONSCIOUS MINDS

We have briefly discussed self-hypnosis and mass hypnosis, the collective unconscious, positive outcomes, and conscious choices. More and more people have been integrating the superconscious aspect into their lives. Here is the way it works.

1. The conscious mind is the director.
2. The conscious mind raises its vibration to call upon the superconscious to influence higher thoughts and emotions.
3. The conscious director can then direct the unconscious mind through higher thought and emotions, affirmations, self-hypnosis or, through enlightened invocation, seek the assistance of the God-Force.
4. Spiritual Hypnotherapists working with the God-Force can help considerably in this instance.
5. Remember when you command it correctly, <u>your unconscious mind is your best friend</u> for it will give you exactly what you programme it to give you.

A synthesis of Love, Wisdom, and Power creates
Mastery – that perfect balance
Between creative thought and feeling in action!

SUPER EMPOWERED CHILDREN

Would you treat your own child the same way
you treat your inner child?

By integrating the sacred trinity of your divine self, embodying it, and acting wisely, allows you to be a huge support not only to those around you, but also to your inner child – that part of you that plays up occasionally, wants attention and sometimes displays 'adult' tantrums as a means of being heard. That part of you that has always sought love outside of yourself.

Tough love means creating boundaries of security for your children; so too first and foremost must you create a 'Fort Knox' of love, security, and boundaries for your inner child.

There are beautiful healing processes to assist in reconnecting with your inner child, incorporating forgiveness, acceptance, attachment cutting and reconnecting with eternal love.

<u>For just five minutes per day</u>, if you continue to practice long, full, deep breathing whilst connecting with your inner love and power and imagining the colourful 'mana' from Heaven; science has proven you will not only improve your intellect, but you will also improve your health and sense of self-worth. You will begin the process of harmonising the amygdala in your brain.

In my hypnotherapy and energy healing practice, I have expanded on these basic Heart Math techniques for over a decade. Some of the case studies are miraculous.

One example I recall is a young eight-year-old boy who was struggling to read in front of the class at school. He presented as distraught, withdrawn, and afraid.

During his first session he was able to witness the changes he could make in his Heart Rate Variability through sending his own love through a Heart Math game on my computer. His attitude changed when he realised his own self-empowerment.

Under my guidance, he completed the game with 100% results in a matter of minutes.

I was delighted to receive a call from his mum the next day. He had read thirty pages in front of the class. How is that for improved self-esteem after one session? Children are magic!

Imagine if we could teach our children skills such as breathing, the Golden Egg, self-reflection, emotional regulation, and positive thinking. It would provide them with valuable tools for understanding and managing their thoughts and emotions. It would foster healthy coping mechanisms, effective communication, and critical thinking skills.

Introducing meditation and relaxation techniques to children can help them develop stress management skills and build resilience in a challenging world.

The more parents that are educated in this work, the more it will 'rub off' on our younger generation and improve the outlook for their future. What would be the compounding effects?

Better relationships, clearer communication techniques, respect for each other and a transcending world of compassion and care. As you are now aware, each person has great influence.

Creative Energy
In its undefined form
Is sculpted by mind
in its everyday norm.

The tough love you give to the child within
The forgiveness you have for the perception of sin.

SUPERPOWERS

With all your gifts you can make a choice
Being true to yourself will release your voice.

Your acts of compassion for one and all.
Unleashes your power to stand mighty and tall.
The willingness you have to stay in your power
Are the choices you make each moment...
Every second, every hour.

When you think thoughts to thrive, believe and know it too!
You have the key to mastering all that you do.

But when you allow your mind to wander
To unconsciously drift and go asunder
into thoughts of fear, judgement, and strife
You begin the process of destroying your life.

It's over to you to infuse thoughts with life
To colour them with love
Or darken them with strife?

Energy makes form
Einstein knew
The quality of Spirit
Creates the view.

CHAPTER SEVENTEEN

THE BALANCING ACT

You are on Earth to learn to balance the feminine and masculine parts of yourself. And you are here to balance the heavenly and earthly aspects of yourself. You are also here to balance your four bodies (physical, mental, soul, spirit) and all your energy chakras – as well as numerous other aspects of yourself that have not been mentioned yet, such as your light quotient.

You are not on Earth to balance the darkness of
negative ego consciousness
with the enlightened love, wisdom, and power of your innate
divine qualities.

You are here to die to the negative ego and
embody the highest ideal consciousness possible in this lifetime.
Heaven is a state of consciousness!

THE JOURNEY FOR EARTHLINGS

The journey toward mastery on Earth extends far beyond the confines of this book. Its essence lies in achieving balance and synthesis, aiming to shed light on the crucial imperative for each individual to actively contribute to the spiritual transformation of both their own physical existence and the entirety of matter encompassing the planet.

Earth, when viewed within the broader cosmic perspective, stands as a planet with a 'developmental lag'. Humanity, as Earthlings, holds a pivotal role within the intricate web of the Galactic body, Solar body and beyond.

If humanity were to comprehend its purpose and propel itself forward, a collective enthusiasm would emerge, breaking free from karmic constraints and propelling the advancement of the planet.

This progression would unveil the subsequent stage in our evolutionary journey. Unfortunately, the prevailing reality is that contemporary mankind is generally adrift, lacking a clear understanding of its direction and the profound meaning of life.

ASCENDING YOUR CONSCIOUSNESS TO MASTERY

Becoming a genuine Master is a profound and multifaceted journey that extends beyond mere proficiency in consciousness. It necessitates a comprehensive understanding and mastery of the intricate dynamics encompassing multiple levels of initiation. However, the journey does not conclude there; it also demands the anchoring and manifestation of your spiritual mission on Earth.

Certain skills, such as channelling, psychic abilities, knowledge in spiritual science, teaching, healing, or clairvoyance, do not inherently denote mastery.

THE BALANCING ACT

True mastery surpasses mere acquisition of individual talents; it demands comprehensive cultivation across three essential dimensions: spiritual, consciousness, and physical/earthly realms. It necessitates the integration of diverse elements, encompassing energy chakras, light rays, Sephiroth of the Tree of Life, twelve archetypes, and the myriad teachings, institutions, and trials encountered throughout life's journey. Such mastery represents a harmonious fusion, transcending the limitations of isolated skills and embracing the interconnectedness of existence in its entirety.

Unfortunately, a prevalent misunderstanding exists where individuals mistakenly identify those possessing singular or combined spiritual gifts as Masters. In reality, a considerable number of individuals endowed with such gifts may be misguided.

The lack of spiritual discernment among the public often results in an unwarranted attribution of power to fragmented and disintegrated 'false prophets and false teachers' – the proverbial wolves in sheep's clothing. Hence the encouragement to practice discernment in all you undertake.

HOW DO YOU EAT AN ELEPHANT? ONE CHUNK AT A TIME.

Initiations are a spiritual process on your evolutionary journey. There are more complexities but to keep it simple in this context, here are the main chunks to proceed with within the third, fourth and fifth dimensions of consciousness.

The initiation process has roots that extend nearly as far back as humanity itself, and it has been conveyed in various forms long before the advent of Christianity. While the concept has taken diverse expressions over time, predating Christianity, the life of Christ stands out as a well-known representation in the New Testament. It serves as a guiding example for humanity, illustrating the pathway to return home to Source, often referred to as Mother/Father God.

CHUNK ONE: The First Initiation – The Birth at Bethlehem

The birth of the Christ on earth symbolises the initial spiritual initiation within the cave of the heart. It involves cultivating foundational mastery over the densest aspect of your being – <u>the physical body</u>. Successfully navigating this initiation demands the development of an introductory level of control over the body, encompassing its appetites, basic needs, sexual impulses, sleep patterns, and more. This endeavour is undertaken in service to the higher self, which, at this juncture, embodies the principles of balance and moderation as its ultimate ideals.

CHUNK TWO: The Second Initiation – The Baptism

The second phase of initiation revolves around attaining mastery over the second densest aspect of your being—<u>the emotional or astral body</u>, symbolised by the baptism of Jesus by John the Baptist. Successfully completing this stage necessitates the cultivation of a level of control over your emotions and desires. This mastery is pursued with the overarching goal of serving the Soul (the intermediary between physical and spiritual) by transforming yourself into an agent of your own destiny, rather than remaining a passive victim to the whims of desires and emotions. This is the most common level of 'stuckness' and is the hardest initiation to graduate. This represents the next rung up the ladder to fourth dimensional consciousness which is the aim of this book.

CHUNK THREE: The Third Initiation – The Transfiguration

The third phase of initiation focuses on mastering the next dense vehicle – <u>the mental body</u>. To successfully navigate this initiation, you must attain a level of control over your mind and thoughts, all in service to the soul. This marks a significant milestone, as it leads to what is known as 'soul merger' or soul infusion – the <u>first major initiation</u>. This is symbolised by the transfiguration of Jesus on the Mount of Olives.

Mastery achieved over the physical body, astral body, and now the mental body enables your earthly personality to unite with its soul on Earth. This transformative process is evident in a growing desire to embody love, forgiveness, and a commitment to service, initiating the gradual liberation from the cycle of rebirth, herewith referred to as 'Karma' or the 'Wheel of Rebirth.'

> *Chunk Three is the limit to where this book looks*
> *But to save your from waiting on tenterhooks*
> *Chunks four, and more open the door*
> *To show you more of what we all look for.*
> *'One chunk at a time'*

CHUNK FOUR: The Fourth Initiation – The Crucifixion or The Great Renunciation

Symbolised by Jesus dying on the cross. In the East it is called the Great Renunciation, where everything is renounced, even life itself if necessary to demonstrate the lifting out of matter into the radiance of the Light of Spirit.

Upon achieving the merging with your soul at the third initiation, a rapid acceleration in your spiritual journey ensues. The fourth initiation stands as a pivotal milestone, marked by the profound transformation of the soul body, also known esoterically as the causal body.

During this initiation, the Higher Self or soul, which has been your guiding force throughout multiple incarnations, undergoes a merging back into the Monad or Spirit. The Monad, alternatively referred to as the 'Mighty I AM Presence' or God-self in certain spiritual traditions, now becomes your guide and teacher, superseding the role previously held by the soul.

The soul body, or causal body, preceding this initiation acts as the repository for all the positive karma accumulated from your past and present lives. This reservoir undergoes a gradual consumption over time as you progress towards the completion of this initiation.

Prior to undertaking this step, you must, to some extent, renounce or relinquish all attachments to the material world. This involves letting go of attachments to fame, fortune, money, power, selfishness, individuals, family, or reputation. Each initiation bestows an increasing amount of energy made up of sub-atomic light particles upon the initiate.

CHUNK FIVE: The Fifth Initiation – The Resurrection

The resurrection of Jesus' body on the third day serves as a symbolic representation of the Resurrection initiation. This transformative process signifies the beginning experience of the liberation of the individual, now a Master, from the enduring influence of material constraints. The Master, having undergone this initiation, possesses at least a 75% light quotient in their being.

CHUNKS SIX AND SEVEN AND BEYOND: Ascension and Strengthening

The sixth and seventh initiations strengthen the 'Monadic merger' or Spirit merge. The sixth is the actual ascension process, whereas the seventh is a strengthening. While outwardly appearing perfectly normal, akin to anyone else's physical form, your body radiates light when viewed esoterically. Only a quarter of your body's atomic structure remains truly atomic, with the rest being composed of sub-atomic elements.

ASCENDED MASTERY

The group of highly evolved beings, known as **'Ascended Masters,'** have transcended duality, illusion, the lower self, fear, and negative ego. By freeing themselves from the cycle of reincarnation, they now serve the Creator and actively guide humanity's evolution toward a prototype state of Beingness.

The term 'Ascended Master' reflects the mastery of self, as you elevate your vibration and achieve ascension in an integrated and balanced manner. This also involves incorporating the light resonance of your initiations into your mind, emotional state, and physical body. In this essence, you are spiritualising matter.

Ascended Masters, existing on the inner spiritual planes, were once embodied on Earth, sharing relatable experiences with individuals today. They have successfully navigated the tests and lessons that everyone on Earth faces, making them familiar figures acting as co-pilots within the Spiritual Hierarchy of Planet Earth. Additionally, there are Ascended Masters at various levels, including Planetary, Solar, Galactic, Universal, and Cosmic, each contributing to the greater cosmic tapestry.

Subtly those Ascended Masters who choose to remain on Earth may continue the evolution of another 15 initiations while leading and overseeing the evolution of others. Some Ascended Masters choose to venture to higher planets or beyond the confines of this cosmic system. This is the beginning of a new adventure, and the process of learning is not complete. It is an eternal unfolding.

Living as an Ascended Master on earth in this state gives liberation from the limitations of the physical realm, no longer bound by the necessity to incarnate. Your body is completely transfigured and resurrected in the esoteric sense.

UNFETTERING THE CHAINS OF REBIRTH

Each step of accomplishing the initial four chunks commences the gradual release of karmic chains, leading to spiritual liberation. This focus is encapsulated by the book's tagline: *"How to Bust Your Karma Through the Invisible Landscape of Your Soul."*

Each initiation phase presents tests, guiding individuals to stabilise at the next higher plane. On Earth, we interact with seven initial planes and nine dimensions. Ascension occurs when your earthly personality, soul, and Spiritual Monad or God-self merge into one unified being, known as the Mighty I AM presence, reflecting an individualised spark of God.

This presence is a co-creative expression within the macrocosm, embodying Love, Light, Wisdom, and Power from Source.

VERTICAL AND HORIZONTAL BALANCE

Spiritual psychology also emphasises maintaining a harmonious balance both vertically and horizontally in life. The vertical plane involves your connection to God and the Masters, while the horizontal plane pertains to relationships with people and Earthly existence. Unfortunately, some Lightworkers emphasise the vertical plane at the expense of the horizontal, while others do the opposite.

Furthermore, spiritual psychology delves into the integration of the mystic and occult aspects within oneself. Individuals may lean more towards mysticism or occultism, but the goal is to harmoniously integrate both aspects to reach their highest potential.

An additional focal point in spiritual psychology involves effectively parenting the inner child. Achieving this entails adopting an attitude of firmness and unconditional love. When this balance is struck, the inner child develops into a well-adjusted individual. Conversely, an imbalance can lead to the inner child growing up with issues related to self-love and self-worth or manifesting rebellious and spoiled behaviours.

Wise action comes from your heart's love-space
Intending the effect of emitting God's grace.
If it lands in a way that isn't ok,
The gift opens mind to a new higher way.
It effects a new cause to open new doors;
To discover new gifts to empower new cause.

"Until we make the unconscious conscious,
it will direct our lives and we will call it 'fate'."
(Carl Jung)

CHAPTER EIGHTEEN

THE FICKLE FACES OF FEAR

The opposite of Love is said to be fear
However there is a place in life for fear.

FEAR – THE SCIENCE

When you experience fear, your autonomic nervous system, which is responsible for regulating various bodily functions, including the parasympathetic and sympathetic nervous systems, plays a crucial role. Your parasympathetic nervous system is generally associated with rest and relaxation. Its activation helps to maintain homeostasis (your body's natural mechanism for healing itself). It conserves energy, promotes digestion, sleep, and other restorative processes.

When in your natural love-based essence, there is scientific evidence your body will experience higher immunity from disease. However, when you feel fear or perceive a threat, your sympathetic nervous system becomes dominant and triggers your body's 'fight-or-flight' response. It stimulates the release of stress hormones like adrenaline and cortisol from the adrenal glands. These hormones prepare your body for action by increasing heart rate, blood pressure, and respiration.

At the same time, your sympathetic nervous system inhibits the parasympathetic activity, reducing its influence on bodily functions.

This inhibition leads to changes such as decreased digestion, reduced salivation, constriction of blood vessels in the skin and internal organs, and relaxation of the bladder and bowel muscles. These physiological changes help redirect your body's resources towards survival-oriented functions, allowing you to respond to the perceived threat effectively.

In summary, when confronted with fear, your parasympathetic nervous system where your happy hormones reside, takes a backseat to the sympathetic nervous system, which becomes dominant and prepares your body for a fight-or-flight response. When fear dominates daily living, it can lead to chronic stress, anxiety, ill health, and a diminished quality of life.

NECESSARY OR INTUITIVE FEAR – THE EXPERIENCE

Although it is often said that fear is the opposite of Love, fear does have a place in your survival. Fear plays a crucial role in keeping you safe by triggering your survival instincts and alerting you to potential threats. It serves as a natural response to danger and helps you take necessary precautions to protect yourself.

By activating the fight-or-flight response, fear can enhance your awareness, sharpen your senses, and prompt you to take immediate action when faced with imminent harm. In this way, fear acts as an innate mechanism that aids in your self-preservation and ensures your physical and emotional well-being.

When experiencing intuitive fear, often referred to as that gut feeling or instinct, your body can exhibit physical reactions. These reactions are commonly associated with the activation of the sympathetic nervous system, which prepares you for fight or flight response as mentioned above.

Some physical responses to intuitive fear may include:

Increased heart rate: Your heart beats faster to pump blood and oxygen to the muscles, preparing your body for action.

Heightened senses: Your senses, such as vision and hearing, may become more acute, allowing for better detection of potential threats.

Muscle tension: Your body may experience increased muscle tension due to the release of stress hormones like adrenaline.

Dilated pupils: Your pupils may dilate to allow more light in, enhancing visual perception.

Hairs standing on end: Sometimes referred to as 'hackles up' or piloerection; this response causes the hair on your body to stand on end and you experience goosebumps. It is an involuntary reaction related to the fight-or-flight response and can make a person appear larger or more threatening.

These physical reactions are part of your innate survival mechanism and can occur when you sense a potential danger or threat. They serve to prepare and optimise your body for quick action or heightened awareness in response to intuitive or perceived threats.

CONSTANT FIGHT OR FLIGHT

If you are in constant stress or fear, such as coping with an abusive relationship or living in constant danger, you may begin to subsist in a place of 'fight-or-flight' which disrupts your body's natural rhythms and may eventually become your norm. This state can also lead into overwhelming feelings.

Similarly, past trauma, often resulting in repetitive aberrations, memories, and nightmares, frequently leads to a diagnosis of Post-Traumatic Stress Disorder (PTSD). Obviously 'prevention is better than cure.' However it is acknowledged that is not the case for the majority of individuals suffering PTSD. Serious health problems often ensue and seeking professional help sooner rather than later is advisable.

UNNECESSARY OR DELUSIONARY FEAR

While fear can be beneficial in certain situations, unnecessary or delusionary fear can also have detrimental effects on your health and wellbeing. If fear dominates your life, it can lead to chronic stress, anxiety, powerlessness, and a diminished quality of life.

Constant fear can inhibit personal growth, limit your ability to take risks, and hinder meaningful connections with others. It may also result in avoidance behaviours and a restricted lifestyle, preventing you from fully experiencing and enjoying life. It is important to recognise and address excessive fear to maintain a healthy balance and well-being.

PAPER TIGERS

Skewed thoughts and learned behaviours can produce fearful emotions often labelled as 'paper tigers.' The term 'paper tigers' is used to describe something that appears threatening or formidable but is not as dangerous or powerful as it seems. It implies that the perceived threat is exaggerated or lacks substance upon closer examination.

In the context of fear and anxiety, considering something as a paper tiger means recognising that the fear is disproportionate to the actual level of danger. It suggests that the perceived threat is not as significant or real as your anxious mind might make it out to be.

When you learn to recognise these fears as paper tigers, you can gain perspective and can challenge their validity. Being able to confront and overcome irrational fears, enables you to live with less anxiety and navigate through life's challenges more effectively.

My Example of a Paper Tiger

Despite nurturing a secret dream of standing on stage and teaching people how to use their minds for self-healing, I harboured an overwhelming fear of public speaking. The mere thought of capturing anyone's attention induced intense anxiety and dread within me. Imagined scenarios of embarrassment, like forgetting my words or facing harsh judgment, haunted my mind.

When prompted for my opinion, my trembling mouth failed to articulate the thoughts in my head. The root cause, I later realised, lay in my struggle with self-love and self-acceptance, prerequisites for standing confidently in my own power. I was trapped in a cycle of fear.

ASTRAL

My dream wasn't working so I asked myself 'why?'
What is the reason? I'm not going to die!
I knew that somewhere within my mind
If I dug deep enough, the answers I'd find.

I didn't like being mocked you see.
It seemed people always made fun of me.
If it wasn't my questions, it was my hair,
Fluffy and fuzzy and full of air.

I remember Anniversary Day when I was three.
Down the hill we went, the whole family.
To the pier that was near
A space for joy, not fear.

Over the side of the boat ramp Mum dangled me,
My feet splashing in the cool green sea.
But she suddenly slipped and dropped me free.
And under the skidway the tide took me.

I bobbed up once and my head hit the wood.
Down again I went; it wasn't so good!
Help me! Help me! There is no air.
Water fills the space where air should be there.

Twice it happened. I gurgled and gasped
The third time up there were hands that grasped.
Up on the deck I was traumatised.
There was water in my lungs and salt in my eyes.

But laughter rang out from all around.
The effect it caused was quite profound.
I didn't know then when I was dropped in the tide.
How the laughing affected my three-year-old pride.

THE FICKLE FACES OF FEAR

Their laughs of relief that I didn't drown.
Set up patterns of belief that I was just a clown.
If I hold the attention; they're going to make fun.
The patterns – they repeated; far more than one.

Some of my colleagues have seen this of me.
Some of them too have encouraged me through.
Lisa Nichols, Vicky, Kate, and others too.
Please know this; I am grateful to you.

My dream is now working so I asked myself 'why?'
What is the reason I didn't die?
'She killed the lion' my mother would say.
'That's the main thing at the end of the day.'

But at the end of the day, friends would relay
<u>'It wasn't the lion that lay dead beside her.</u>
<u>It was nothing at all but a squashed paper tiger!'</u>

How To Squash a Paper Tiger

When confronted with challenges, choose to face them with a positive outcome in mind. Remember, you're not going to die; you are going to inspire!

Take public speaking as an example. Many share the 'paper tiger' fears I experienced. Often, people are relieved it is you up there and not them. As you deliver your presentation, you will realise the fear was unfounded and exaggerated. Passion for your topic turns that fear into wisdom.

With practice, each presentation becomes an opportunity to refine your strategy. However, obsessive focus on negative scenarios can trigger the Law of Correspondence: 'As within, so without.' Continual focus on what you resist might bring about the very affects you fear. The pattern may persist until you learn the lesson, possibly even through reincarnation.

Remember, what you resist, persists! Refer to the RAS within the brain.

> The first thing to do to make a good start,
> is take three full breaths through the love in your heart.
> Breathe all the way through as <u>aqua blue</u>,
> This type of breathing clears the fear from you.
>
> Your neural links will spark so bright.
> And light up your brain for a new insight.
> Keep the intention true for all to win
> And soon you'll knock that fear on the chin!

The soothing colour of aqua blue is associated with the Light Ray emanating from your Heart Centre of Loving Wisdom and Understanding. Symbolising truth, devotion, calmness, self-expression, and sincerity, this colour aids in enhancing the natural integration of your Soul and promoting higher mental clarity.

By stimulating spontaneous healing through the power of Love, it positively influences your mental, emotional, and physical well-being, aligning with the Light of the Soul. Additionally, it plays a role in healing mental self-criticism and fear.

Unconscious Fear Patterns

Patterns of fear, based on earlier traumatic experiences can manifest in various ways and to varying degrees from PTSD to phobias, feelings of not being good enough, ill health and a whole range of anxieties; some of them rooted in past life experiences.

Here is another example to illustrate how past traumas can influence fear patterns: Suppose you experienced a traumatic event in your childhood, such as a dog bite. This event left a deep emotional impact and created an association between dogs and fear.

As a result, you may develop a fear of dogs, known as a 'specific phobia.' In your adult life, encountering dogs or even the thought of being near them can trigger intense anxiety and panic. Your body may exhibit physical reactions such as a racing heart, sweating, and hypervigilance. This fear response is a result of the traumatic experience and the subsequent repetitive conditioning that has occurred.

In this scenario, the fear pattern is deeply rooted in your past traumatic experience. The association between dogs and fear becomes ingrained, and your mind and body automatically react to even the thought of dogs as if they pose a significant threat.

> *'It's not the pain that Is bothering one;*
> *it Is the thought of the pain that bothers one.*
> *It's not the situation that one is troubled with,*
> *but the fear of the situation that Is troubling one.'*
> *... Sri Sri Ravi Shankar, 'Realising We Are Spirit.'*

Within The Law of Polarity fear-based emotions, stresses, anxieties, and anger are the opposite to love based emotions. They are of the same vital energy but have been 'thought formed' and trained by reactions to experiences to remain at the lower and depleting end of the 'pole.' If you are constantly in stress and fear, I encourage you to seek professional help.

Triggers

Your body was not designed to attack itself. By your thoughts and emotions, you can create optimum health and joy; or anxiety and dis-ease. Being healthy and well is the inherent birthright of everyone. Utilising uncomfortable reactions as consciousness 'triggers' can guide you in discovering your innate gifts and support your return to grace.

If you struggle with these attitudinal healing techniques, seek help from a professional who is experienced in these matters. Use your discernment when making a choice. Your physical, emotional, mental, and spiritual energy systems have an inbuilt immune system which you deserve to enjoy.

Under the Natural Law of Vibration,
your body becomes the mirror of the energy that feeds its potential.

Seven Stress Busting Tips:

1. Heart based breathing exercises as outlined within this book.
2. Identify the sources of stress – focus on a solution and act upon it.
3. Eliminate unhealthy ways of dealing with stress, including reactive behaviours, poor dietary choices, alcohol, and drug dependency, among others.
4. Get moving – regular exercise can help balance your nervous system and increase blood flow – walking in nature is therapeutic.
5. Connect with others – social support can help you manage stress.

6. Make time for fun and relaxation – hobbies and leisure activities can help you unwind.
7. Manage your time better – prioritise your tasks and delegate when possible.

It is important to take care of yourself and seek help if you need it. You don't have to go through stress alone.

WHERE TO SEEK HELP

Recognising and addressing emotional patterns early is crucial, offering the power of choice before situations worsen. Seeking support, such as attitudinal healing, is recommended over resorting to medications or anti-depressants. Hypnotherapy, often seen as a last resort, can serve as a preventative method, supporting emotional health and attitude.

It's advised to seek a professional hypnotherapist affiliated with a reputable association early on, not only to alleviate stress on the traditional health system but also to potentially eliminate the need for medication. Addressing issues at the unconscious level can prevent the escalation of fear or anger and subsequent physical disease. If physical illness arises, consulting a doctor is essential; hypnotherapy can serve as additional support.

"What isn't dealt with on the front end will metastasise into an ugly morass of dysfunction and eventually losses."
(Dan Wolken)

While modern hypnotherapy has demonstrated significant success with positive outcomes, formal recognition as a vital contributor to holistic health remains elusive from governments and traditional health authorities worldwide. This hesitancy persists despite its effectiveness in crucial areas such as smoking cessation, performance enhancement, and stress management, including the metaphysical embodiments of stress.

Notably, numerous well-known figures, including Albert Einstein, Mozart, Nikola Tesla, Thomas Edison, Winston Churchill, Tiger Woods, Princess Diana, and Jackie Onassis, have sought the aid of hypnotherapy. The fact that these individuals, with access to the world's top personal development resources, choose hypnosis speaks volumes.

Considered an extra edge in unlocking talents, overcoming limitations, and attracting success, hypnosis offers a unique approach to personal growth. Its roots trace back to ancient Egyptian times, marking a rich history of transformative practices.

Significant research and ethical advancements have evolved since the era of Frans Mesmer, the Father of mesmerism, and James Braid, the British Surgeon and pioneer of medical applications in hypnotherapy in the 1700s.

Embracing the transformative power of hypnosis might just be the catalyst you need for your onward journey.

CHAPTER NINETEEN

DIMENSIONS AND DENSITIES

Dimensions represent different aspects or facets of reality that coexist within the ALL; often layered or intersecting. Dimensions can encompass various planes of existence, each with its own set of laws and characteristics, and are not solely tied to vibrational frequencies.

Densities refer to the level of vibrational resonance or energy concentration in a particular plane of existence. Higher densities are associated with more refined or elevated states of consciousness and spiritual awareness.

DELUSIONS OF THE ASTRAL PLANE
The Purpose of These Writings

These writings delve into the astral plane, representing the emotional body of mass egoic consciousness. Within this realm, we confront the lower astral plane characterised by a collective unconsciousness entrenched in fear-based emotions stemming from humanity's negative ego.

Here, the astral realm presents a spectrum ranging from lower tiers akin to religious concepts such as 'purgatory,' where fragmented souls grapple with separation, fear, and terror, to higher regions hosting common dream states, out-of-body experiences, and lucid dreaming.

The discussion often revolves around negative entities including ghosts, poltergeists, or negative extra-terrestrials, influencing humans. While encounters with these entities may be perceived as dreams or illusions in elevated states of consciousness; they can pose genuine and perilous threats to the unaware and unprotected.

The crux lies in the understanding that alignment of vibrations with illusory entities occurs when consciousness descends to the level of the astral/emotional plane.

Working in this field as a therapist presents challenges, underscoring the importance of prevention and self-responsibility.

In contrast to secular or spiritually untrained practices of conscious astral travel, the hierarchy of ascended masters advises against venturing into this realm. Instead, they advocate for journeys into the higher realms of consciousness, equivalent to the light of the soul. Preparation in a state of grace and protection is paramount before embarking on such journeys, ensuring safe passage to dimensions where supportive and healing entities offer profound wisdom.

Thus, maintaining a state of grace before sleep and during conscious travel to higher dimensions becomes imperative to transcend the delusions of the astral plane and navigate the realms of pure, elevated consciousness.

WHY MIND PROTECTION?

We have established that ALL is mental; our mind creates our reality. Some earthlings mistakenly believe that mind protection is unnecessary, falsely embracing a 'subjective truth' that they are already living their life in their highest, wisest, most powerful plane of existence, often manifesting as 'power over' others. It is a trick of the ego to think you are invulnerable to the conglomerate of dark energies that exists on the lower astral plane.

When on your earthly evolutionary journey, mind protection is a necessary component of everyday life. Consider the prevalent mass mental health issues and the existence of a dark brotherhood of confused souls who prioritise self over all, exploiting and using others for selfish gain.

Is it not better to err on the side of caution? Is it not preferable to live in a semipermeable egg of God's golden light than absorb other people's negative thought manifestations?

Use your power of discernment to question any teachings or beliefs suggesting otherwise. Is there another agenda operating?

To whom or what are you giving your innate power away?

In effect your absorbent unconscious mind faces the imperative to safeguard its energy field, particularly in a world of global chaos, vulnerable states like sleep or when grappling with negative emotions. In this, I include leaders, teachers, parents; in fact, all who care.

ASTRAL

A DAMAGED OZONE LAYER

The need for protection extends to instances involving mind-altering substances in any form, where altered states of consciousness can potentially expose individuals to a broader spectrum of energies on both the physical and astral planes.

During these vulnerable moments, the unguarded mind may inadvertently attract or be susceptible to negative influences, some of which can attach themselves to the etheric body and live vicariously off its energy. Thus, the practice of shielding your energy field becomes crucial as it acts as a barrier against unwanted intrusions and ensures a more harmonious engagement with the various planes of existence.

The analogy of blowing a hole in your personal ozone layer (similar to what fluorocarbons do to the earth's atmosphere) can be applied to individuals struggling with drug addiction or alcoholism, where personalities undergo significant changes 'under the influence', suggesting other more sinister energies at play, for example:

Fluctuating Moods and Aggression: Substance abuse can lead to extreme mood swings, with individuals oscillating between euphoria and deep despair. In a manner analogous to environmental damage, the consistent use of drugs or alcohol may erode emotional stability, causing sudden outbursts of anger or aggression that are out of character for the person.

Impaired Judgment and Decision-Making: Similar to the impact of environmental pollutants, substance abuse can create cognitive 'holes' in one's ability to make sound judgments. Individuals may engage in risky behaviours, make impulsive decisions, and display a lack of foresight or consideration for consequences.

Isolation and Alienation: The personal ozone layer, in this context, can be seen as a protective barrier against negative influences. Substance abuse often leads to the breakdown of relationships and social connections, isolating individuals from their support networks. This isolation can contribute to a changed personality characterised by withdrawal, secrecy, and a focus solely on obtaining and using the substance.

Loss of Authentic Self: Continuous substance abuse can lead to a gradual erosion of one's authentic personality, akin to the depletion of the ozone layer. The individual may adopt a persona driven by the need to sustain their addiction, hiding their true self behind a façade of dependency.

Inability to Cope with Reality: Individuals struggling with addiction may use substances as a coping mechanism, creating a hole in their ability to face and address life's challenges without relying on external substances. This coping deficit can result in a distorted personality that relies heavily on the temporary relief provided by drugs or alcohol.

In essence, the analogy highlights how the protective layers of a person's character can be compromised by the destructive influence of substance abuse, leading to significant changes in behaviour, cognition, and overall personality.

Anyone, particularly those suffering with undiagnosed post-traumatic stress disorder (PTSD), who resists addressing their emotions, may find themselves at a heightened risk of turning to substance abuse as a means of coping with the unaddressed psychological distress; thus laying themselves bare to other destructive forces.

DENSITIES OF VIBRATION

Within the tapestry of existence, every element of nature resonates with a unique and subtle energy, from the majestic mountains to the humblest pebble. Even the air we breathe, the waters that flow, the earth beneath our feet, and the fire that warms us pulsate with vibrant vitality. As stewards entrusted with dominion over the Earth, it is our privilege and responsibility to harmonise with and nurture this sacred bond.

By immersing ourselves in pristine natural environments, free from the pollution and debris of human intervention, we attune our vibrations to the timeless rhythms and innate energies of creation. In these sanctuaries, we reconnect with the essence of our birthright, aligning our spirits with the ancient wisdom and boundless vitality of the Earth.

Our role is to consciously direct, anchor, and sustain our thoughts, actions, and emotions in accordance with this profound interconnectedness. By doing so, we contribute to the well-being of all life forms, fostering harmony and balance within the intricate web of existence.

As we honour and respect the sanctity of nature and its Laws, we honour and uplift ourselves, recognising that in nurturing the world around us, we ultimately nurture the deepest essence of our own souls.

Vibrational Densities:
I have underscored the densities on which this book is mainly focused for these are the areas that humanity in general needs to address to begin diminishing past karma and co-create holistic healing in the global sense. The vibrational densities are vast in number, so I have taken the first seven as an example in this context.

DIMENSIONS AND DENSITIES

Level	Vibrational Density
1st	Mineral kingdom
2nd	Plant and lower animal kingdom
3rd	Higher animal and <u>lower human</u>
4th	<u>Low: Astral, lower emotional realms</u>
4th	<u>High: Etheric, higher mental realms</u>
5th	<u>Low: Causal, creative realms</u>
5th	High: Soul
6th	Oversoul
7th	Master oversoul, Atmic Plane

MULTI-DIMENSIONAL CONSCIOUSNESS

"In my Father's House, there are many mansions."
(Jesus Christ, New Testament, John 14:2)

Dimensions of consciousness represent various levels of awareness and perception, each reflecting a different internal state of consciousness. It's important to note that individuals can operate from multiple dimensions simultaneously.

The first four dimensions are often associated with humanity's experience of egoic duality. Real love, considered a higher form of consciousness, is said to begin at the fifth dimension. While this overview is simplified, it provides a glimpse into the complexity of consciousness, referred to here as the *'Father's Many Mansions.'*

Dimensions of Consciousness:

Here is a brief example of each dimension up to the seventh, acknowledging that there are numerous dimensions beyond the scope of this discussion each offering unique experiences as catalysts for positive transformation:

Level	State of Consciousness
1D	Existence, non-biological
2D	Instinctual, emotional, animalistic
3D	Intellectual, logical, rational mind, ego (conformity)
4D	Creative, imaginative, realm of cause and effect (individuality)
5D	Pure intelligence, insight, love (spontaneous compassion)
6D	Causal level, soul level (last level of individuality)
7D++	Oversoul level (group consciousness)

THE CRY OF THE PLANET

In the symphony of the natural world, where each element harmonises in an upward spiral of evolution, humanity stands apart, disrupting this sacred rhythm with the discordant notes of negative ego. This disharmony casts a shadow upon the planet, dampening its vibrant resonance.

It is a sobering realisation that, as a global community, we have neglected our duty to nurture and protect the very essence that sustains us – the natural world. Yet, amidst this realisation lies the beacon of hope: the invitation to embark on a journey of self-discovery and self-nurturing.

By tending to the garden of our own souls, we prepare ourselves to join the collective consciousness of nature, humanity, and the Earth itself. For in truth, we are all interconnected, each a unique expression of universal consciousness, traversing multiple dimensions of existence.

When we awaken to our place in the grand tapestry of life and ensure that our thoughts and emotions resonate at their highest frequency, we become catalysts for positive transformation. Just as the vibration of the planet mirrors the collective consciousness of humanity, so too does each individual ripple of uplifted energy contribute to the symphony of existence.

May this awareness guide us toward a future where the cry of the planet is met with the harmonious resonance of awakened souls, united in their commitment to nurture, honour, and uplift all of life.

The Physical: The physical body acts as a conduit for higher vibrations by aligning actions with spiritual values like compassion and harmony. Individual actions ripple out to influence the Earth's energetic vibration, fostering collective evolution and upliftment.

The Etheric Double: Every manifested form has an etheric energy blueprint, akin to an energy battery storing light and heat. Similar to the human body's energy channels, Earth's ley lines and vortexes reflect patterns for energy flow. Congestion in the etheric body can lead to physical vulnerability.

The Astral or Emotional Body: The astral plane mirrors individual desires and emotions, akin to water's fluid nature. Emphasising the need to train the astral body to receive higher impressions promotes serenity and clarity amidst external influences.

The Mental Body: Mastery over positive thoughts diminishes the dominance of emotions, leading to transcendence of illusion and karma. This mastery fosters spiritual evolution and liberation from cycles of reincarnation.

Each aspect highlights the interconnectedness between individual consciousness and the planet's energetic state, underscoring the transformative potential of aligning with higher principles.

**THE ULTIMATE IDEAL OUTCOME
IS TO CREATE HEAVEN ON EARTH**

*"Spiritual growth is just a Band-Aid
which will eventually become corrupted and contaminated*
'IF'
the foundational consciousness of the people of the Earth is run by the emotional body, negative ego, subconscious mind, and inner child. Eventually that consciousness will corrupt everything."
(Extracted from 'Cliff Notes of the Divine Plan'
by Dr Joshua David Stone PhD)

CHAPTER TWENTY

BEST OUTCOMES

Values: Values are beliefs or principles that individuals or societies consider important and hold dear. They are deeply ingrained and guide decision-making, actions, and behaviour. Values provide a framework for evaluating what is right or wrong, desirable, or undesirable, and shape our priorities and choices.

Values can be influenced by cultural, societal, religious, or personal factors. Examples of values include honesty, justice, freedom, equality, family, respect, loyalty, and responsibility. Values can vary from person to person or from one culture to another, but they provide a sense of direction or a driving force to help establish a sense of identity and purpose.

Virtues: Virtues refer to desirable moral qualities or characteristics that individuals possess or cultivate within themselves. They are positive traits or habits of behaviour that contribute to personal growth and ethical conduct. They are seen as embodied and guiding principles for human behaviour.

Some examples of virtues include honesty, integrity, compassion, courage, humility, patience, and generosity. Virtues are cultivated through conscious effort and practice and are considered essential for leading a good and meaningful life.

There are many other values and virtues that people hold. <u>Positive Affirmations</u> are a conscious practice to turn values into virtues. For instance, one of my own values apart from some of those mentioned above, has highly likely become a virtue by now. It is ingrained in me to 'enhance every space I enter' my intent being to add value wherever I find myself, to be my best self, whether it is picking up rubbish on the beach, tidying up clutter, offering support, listening, cheering up someone's day with a big smile. There are many layers to that one virtue that becomes an unconscious trait.

In summary, values are deeply held beliefs and principles that guide behaviour and decision-making. Values have a broad scope and can influence societal norms and expectations. Virtues are personal qualities or character traits that individuals cultivate within themselves.

Virtues are more focused on individual character development. Both virtues and values play important roles in shaping our ethical behaviour and the way we interact with others and the world around us. Perhaps you already know your highest value; some people do not as I have experienced in my Practice.

Determining to always have in mind the best and most ideal outcome for ALL is a process of using your 'highest' values and virtues to train your brain.

- Values are what drives your behaviours.
- Knowing what drives you is of enormous benefit in the process of self-actualising.
- Values are a first step in becoming 'virtuous.'

- Values can be transformed into virtues that become part of your ideal Beingness.
- Suggestions to the unconscious mind can support positive rewiring based on your values and virtues.

Note: *When 'Happiness' is stated as a value it always needs to be explored further. Happiness is subjective. It refers to your personal opinions, interpretations, or experiences and can vary from person to person. It is important to be clear on what makes you happy.*

Self-eliciting answers around 'Happiness':

1. How would you describe happiness in your own words?
2. Can you recall a specific time when you felt genuinely happy? What made that experience special?
3. Who is around? What are you doing?
4. What are the things or activities that bring you joy or a sense of fulfillment?
5. How do you define a meaningful and satisfying life for yourself?
6. Are there any obstacles or challenges that prevent you from experiencing happiness more frequently?
7. What role do your relationships and social connections play in your overall happiness?
8. Are there any specific goals or aspirations that, if achieved, would contribute to your happiness?
9. Are there any values or beliefs that you hold dear that contribute to your sense of happiness?

These questions aim to facilitate clarity on what experiences or beliefs make you feel happy. They may also identify what is making you unhappy.

> When you know what you don't want;
> take the opposite tack and look for <u>what you do want</u>.

Clarifying values provides a good driver for taking a course of positive action. You can always ask your NLP or Hypnotherapy professional to help you elicit your highest values if you are struggling. When they are identified you can turn them into embedded virtues.

SINS OF THE FATHERS

The Sins of the Fathers imply that the consequences of wrongdoing or sin committed by one generation can have an impact on subsequent generations. It suggests a form of intergenerational or inherited karma, where the actions or choices of ancestors have repercussions that extend beyond their own lives and affect their descendants.

The simple example of parents or grandparents using drugs or smoking has the potential to extend to their grandchildren through both genetic mutations and epigenetic modifications, potentially influencing the grandchildren's susceptibility to certain health conditions or behavioural traits.

The scientific understanding of epigenetics reveals how environmental factors, including emotional experiences, can influence gene expression and potentially modify inherited traits. This concept suggests that the present generation holds the power to break the chains of inherited traits by creating supportive emotional environments and making positive lifestyle changes.

Modern epigenetics underscores the interconnectedness of past, present, and future generations while highlighting the potential for resilience and adaptation in the face of inherited predispositions.

Overall, the concept of the 'sins of the fathers' raises important questions about responsibility, justice, and the interconnectedness of past, present, and future generations. It reminds us of the complex ways in which our actions can shape the world not just today, but for generations to come.

We established the Sacral Chakra as being related to the seven cardinal sins. Although not widely expressed, modern metaphysics has drawn connections between an association of the seven cardinal sins with corresponding chakras – the topic for another conversation.

MISTAKES

"OOOOW!"

I am dragging myself across the floor towards the kitchen desperately hoping the telephone has been connected. The pain is intense. I am alone in the little country cottage that is to become my home. Every inch is agony. There is no way I can stand. I reach the kitchen door and pull at the cord yanking the telephone to the ground. Eureka! The line is alive. 111 is the emergency number in New Zealand. I dial it.

"What is your emergency?"

"I need an ambulance!" I gasp.

It is the third week after moving all my belongings to a shed on my recently purchased lifestyle block. I am elated and exhausted at the same time. Moving house and managing a major conference in the South Island within a fortnight of each other is a major ask of myself. But I have been running on adrenaline, determined to achieve.

The little cottage is dotted humbly on the flat top of a sand dune close to the coast and 150 kilometres north of the city where I work. Almost an acre of pretty gardens and tree-covered land alive with the song of tuis, bellbirds, and wood pigeons. I have purchased a weed eater. The land is too steep for a lawnmower. I am fit and strong in my mid-fifties. I have arranged to work from home and take the train into the office once or twice a week.

What is more, I am now within 10 minutes' drive of my sister who suffers from multiple sclerosis. She has always held a special place in my heart, and I am looking forward to sharing lunches and laughter with her. The rest of my family are living their lives in faraway places. I am giving myself a virtual pat on the back. I have worked long and hard for this. It is the first time I have owned and lived in a home I have purchased from the 'sweat of my own brow' and not in partnership with anyone else.

My dream is worth it! I have already planted some white standard roses to enhance the garden in front of the deck. Further possibilities expand my mind. As I unpack, I intensely remove the residual grime of the previous owners. The sun is shining. I have just taken the freshly washed curtains off the clothesline and am focused on rehanging them.

My shoulders ache from arranging furniture and unpacking boxes. As I lift my arms to rehang the curtains, I look around me. The previous owners have left a stepping stool in the lounge.

How synchronistic. Taking my body one step up will help relieve the pain in my shoulders!

BEST OUTCOMES

"Stupid stool!" No wonder they left it behind…

"I think I've broken my leg," I tell the operator. *"My foot is sticking out at right angles."*

Naively, I am hoping my foot may be dislocated; something like when people dislocate their shoulders. I am told to stay where I am. The ambulance will be with me in 20 minutes. At arm's length is my bookshelf containing a few unpacked books. I grab the first one I can reach. It is entitled *'The Complete Pocket Positives'*.

It opens. The message reads:

> *"Even a mistake may turn out to be the one thing necessary to a worthwhile achievement."*
> (Henry Ford)

The impact of this accident halted my momentum and plunged me into the depths of the 'dark night of the soul.' I had been immersed in a bustling life, overseeing conferences nationwide, neglecting my hypnotherapy practice in the process.

Despite numerous warning signs, I pressed forward in my chaotic world, reaping financial rewards and enjoying its benefits. Yet, my true life purpose remained neglected. The dark night stripped me bare.

Eventually, I lost my relationship, job, home, security, and depleted any savings I had. I found myself overwhelmed and in poor health. Resorting to my credit card, I struggled to pay my mortgage until it reached its limit. Drowning in debt, hope seemed distant.

As I navigated the social welfare system in my new circumstances, I encountered shocking anomalies and exploitative practices.

ASTRAL

Despite my efforts to maintain dignity, I found myself treated poorly. Financially destitute and alone, the dark night persisted not for a mere 40 days and 40 nights, but for several agonising years.

When you don't take note of the signs to get back on track
the metaphorical Big Mack Truck will come
along and bowl you over.

CHAPTER TWENTYONE

WHAT EVERYONE IS DYING TO KNOW

There is no such thing as death.
Except for the death of the ugly ego!

When you leave this earthly plane
You will know these words are not insane.
With neither body nor a brain.
There simply is no physical pain.

You are the Eternal creative Mind
What you believe is what you'll find.
Your consciousness will forever endure
Be it sullied with smut or so very pure.

For now, it's such a good idea
To command your way while you are here.

To commence to fill
all space with grace.

ASTRAL

*And prepare your soul
for its spiritual place.*

*If you haven't yet raised the bar
And realised who you truly are.
Then your perception is in error
And death remains a terror.*

*Life doesn't cease.
Ego death gives release.
So prepare while you're here,
For the best adventure out there.*

*And if and when you do return
There won't be so much more to learn.
You can spend your time with grit and nerve
With grace and joy you'll gladly serve.*

*So here, I say again - once more
To break the chains of karmic law
Your mind is the Golden Door
To glorious places you can yet explore.*

DEATH – WHAT HAPPENS?

"Where your consciousness goes when your body dies is determined by the last thought in your mind before death."
(Krishna in the Bhagavad Gita)

Acknowledgements are notably made here to the esoteric writings and channellings of Alice A. Baily and Dr Joshua David Stone, Founder of I AM University, where much of this

WHAT EVERYONE IS DYING TO KNOW

*information has been sourced.
I am just expressing it my way.*

I – EGO DEATH

*Transcending dark ego is a tiny death every day,
Whilst you set in place a divine new way,
To stand in your power, your love, and your light
And gather more wisdom to assume this fight.*

*The road ahead is paved in Gold
When tolerance, forgiveness and love unfold
Being willing to evolve along the way,
You'll light up your path 'til you're old and grey.*

*The practice of 'harmlessness' in all you do
Makes every day fresh and adventurous too.
As you die to the negative parts of you
Each day you meet a newer you!*

II – SLEEP – DEATH

*And every night when you count your sheep
There's a similar death when you're sound asleep.
Your egoic mind it travels elsewhere.
'Willy-nilly-wandering' - where it shouldn't dare.*

*When in the <u>lower</u> Astral it can be found,
You'll twig to my counsel to turn around, and
Weave a gold love-egg 'round you at night,
To hold you safe from many a plight!*

*Practice this nightly with your inner eye
Before the ego goes touring in a darkened sky.
'Why is that?' you may well ask of me.
Alternatively...
The Soul's <u>Higher</u> Planes are a sight to see!
Glorious adventures await you and me.*

*So, take control of your time of rest
Make your dreams a quality of the very best.
For what's in your mind as you drift off at night
Can be a dark place of danger or glorious light!*

MY MOTHER'S REPEATED PRAYER

As a child, every night before bed, my mother would have us say a prayer, instructing us to fold our arms across our chest.

*As I lay me down to sleep
I pray the Lord, my soul to keep.
If I should die before I wake,
I pray the Lord my soul to take.*

The prayer instilled in me a fear of dying before waking up. I could not comprehend how one could wake up after death. Instead of bringing comfort, the prayer triggered unsettling questions and led to many nightmares.

Looking back, I understand that my mother intended to secure the belief that we would go to God if we died in our sleep. However, my young mind struggled to rationalise it, given the conflicting teachings of a God who would take my soul if I died and send me to Hell if I misbehaved.

Growing up in fear of a sky-dwelling, judgmental God with a long grey beard, who knew and saw everything, also made confession to the local priest a scary experience.

In this chaotic age, the concept of a loving and merciful God Source of all love, light, power, and wisdom, makes more sense. Choosing to live in love rather than fear feels like a more supportive and liberating path. The saying, *"Where your consciousness goes when you die is determined by the last thought in your mind before death"*, underscores the importance of being in a state of <u>G</u>race <u>O</u>ver <u>D</u>rama at all times. You never know when your number comes up!

Reflecting on these childhood fears, I wonder if my little soul, during those nights, unknowingly traversed the astral plane of emotions, delving into the conglomerate of man's dark feelings that reside within that murky realm.

III – END-OF-PHYSICAL-LIFE DEATH

Just the same, what happens at the end of your physical life,
Is whether your mind is at peace or in dire strife,
For the last thing you have on your mind,
Determines your journey you will undoubtedly find.

Keeping in your love and your joy and your power
Will nurture and guide you in your death hour.
You get three chances to go to the Light,
So transition with Grace and let go of the fight.

Whether or not you've busted your karma
Merging with the light's glory will lessen the drama.

*And when you return to the Earth next time around
You will find yourself on more hallowed ground.*

DEATH AND REBIRTH

With every death also comes a corresponding rebirth. The processes of initiation are nothing more than death to a certain level of consciousness, and the rebirth a more expansive liberating state. The pain comes only when you are attached to the level you are in.

In the cosmos, there exist realms and dimensions far surpassing our own, inhabited by beings possessing abilities and attributes beyond human imagination. Remarkably, these entities once trod paths akin to ours, yet evolved to heights surpassing our comprehension. Similarly, as individuals, we are destined to transcend our current state, ascending to realms of greater realisation over time, as illuminated teachings profess.

The concept of death, in its relative sense, holds no permanence; rather, it signifies the dawn of a new existence. Our journey extends infinitely, traversing ever-upward through planes of existence for countless epochs.

Within the boundless expanse of the Omniverse, our exploration knows no limits, spanning the farthest reaches within the Infinite Mind of the ALL, where our potential and opportunities stretch across all time and space continuum.

The Kybalion explains:

"When the Grand Cycle of eons draws to its ultimate culmination, the ALL will gather its creations unto itself. In that moment, we shall embrace this union eagerly, attaining a

profound understanding of being one with the ALL. Meanwhile, find solace in the assurance of being safeguarded and nurtured by the Infinite Power of the Father-Mother Mind."

"Within the Father/Mother Mind, mortal children are at home. There is not one who is Fatherless, nor Motherless in the Universe."

THE BARDO EXPERIENCE

The concept of the 'bardo' originates from Tibetan Buddhism and refers to intermediate states between death and rebirth. These intermediate states are believed to be crucial transitional phases where consciousness exists in a state separate from the physical body. There is an art to dying – just as there is an art to living.

1. **The Bardo at the Moment of Death:**
   This phase begins just before the moment of physical death. During this phase, individuals experience a vivid and intense vision of the 'blinding clear light of God.' This clear light represents the ultimate nature of mind and existence. However, most individuals are unable to recognise or fully embrace this luminosity due to habitual attachments and fears. The quality of your consciousness during this phase significantly influences the subsequent stages of the bardo journey.

   In the 'Bhagavad Gita', Krishna stated:

   *"Where you go when you die,
   is the last thought in your mind before you die.
   Let the last thought in your mind be only
   to merge with the Light, to merge with God.
   This can be a death bed Salvation and Liberation."*

Unfortunately, the majority of people worldwide lack education regarding the art and science of death and dying, leaving them unaware of the 'Clear Light of God.'

Consequently, they miss out on this opportunity due to factors such as ignorance, preconceived religious beliefs, or fear of the light. It may also occur that relatives prolong the process or individuals are too heavily medicated to fully experience and embrace this opportunity. The reasons are probably infinite.

As expressed, in the Bhagavad Gita, the merging with this light can possibly mean liberation from the wheel of rebirth: The prodigal son in repentance is welcomed home.

The Second Opportunity:
If a soul misses the initial merging with the 'Clear Light of God' there is another opportunity to merge. The secondary light is toned down and may be more comfortable to some. However, this merging still enables you to gain in your spiritual development.

2. **The Bardo of the Experiencing of Reality:**
If the first two opportunities are missed, during a 3-day period, consciousness undergoes a series of hallucinatory visions and experiences, believed to be reflections of one's past thoughts, actions, and karma. These visions can span a spectrum from blissful to terrifying, contingent upon the individual's spiritual evolution and the nature of their past deeds.

This phase is sometimes referred to as the 'valley of judgment,' not so much in the egoic sense, but rather as a spiritual review of one's life with a newfound clarity not previously experienced. The purpose of these experiences is to offer opportunities for self-awareness, purification, and liberation from the cycle of suffering. <u>It's important to note that these visions are not indicative of divine judgment; rather, the soul is effectively assessing itself in a dream-like state that feels entirely real</u>.

3. **The Bardo of Becoming:** The final phase of the bardo occurs just before rebirth. In this phase, individuals are drawn towards a new rebirth based on their karmic imprints and desires. The experiences of the Bardo of Becoming are likened to dreaming, where individuals may encounter various realms, beings, and potential life situations. The choices made during this phase are believed to influence the conditions and circumstances of the next life.

Liberation from the cycle of rebirth is considered possible through the recognition of the true nature of reality and the cultivation of wisdom and compassion.

ON OTHER PLANES

In various spiritual and metaphysical beliefs, the circumstances and state of mind at the time of death can influence your experiences on different planes of existence. Here's a general perspective on how individuals who die in fear or peacefully, as well as those who commit acts of violence versus those who serve humanity, might experience these planes:

Death in Fear vs Peaceful Death:

Fearful Death: If someone dies in fear, particularly due to traumatic events or at the hands of others, their transition to the afterlife may involve carrying the emotional residue of that fear. In some belief systems, this fear might manifest in the initial stages of the afterlife, influencing the individual's perceptions and experiences until they are guided by angelic beings or other spiritual entities to transcend or resolve it.

Peaceful Death: Conversely, someone who dies peacefully, perhaps after a life well-lived or with a sense of acceptance, may transition to the afterlife with a more serene state of mind. This peaceful transition could contribute to a smoother and more positive experience on the spiritual planes.

Act of Violence vs Service to Humanity

Act of Violence: Individuals who commit acts of violence may face karmic consequences or spiritual challenges in the afterlife. Depending on the belief system, they might encounter the need for spiritual growth, reconciliation, or redemption to move beyond the negative impact of their actions.

Service to Humanity: Those who dedicate their lives to serving humanity, promoting compassion, and contributing positively may experience a more harmonious transition. Their actions may align with higher spiritual principles, potentially leading to a more uplifting and fulfilling existence on the spiritual planes.

Heaven is a state of consciousness comprising many mansions!

THE MECHANICS OF DYING – WHAT HAPPENS?

Not necessarily in this order

1. The removal of the life thread or silver cord.
2. The removal of the consciousness thread.
3. The exit of the three permanent atoms.
4. The exit of etheric astral and mental bodies.
5. The raising of the kundalini and the exit of the personality.

1. **The Removal of the Life Thread or Silver Cord:**
   The life thread, or silver cord, serves as the energetic link between the Mighty I AM presence or Monad and the heart. This shimmering silver connection represents the vital life force sustaining the physical body throughout life, even during soul travel and out-of-body experiences. Upon death, the removal of this cord separates the life force from the physical body.

2. **The Removal of the Consciousness Thread:**
   The consciousness thread symbolises individual awareness or higher consciousness, distinct from the physical body and life force energy. It is depicted as a luminous thread connecting the centre of consciousness to higher spiritual realms. Removal of this thread signifies an expansion of consciousness beyond physical limitations, marking a shift to higher states of awareness often experienced during meditation, spiritual awakening, or near-death experiences.

   <u>Associated with spiritual enlightenment and connection to universal consciousness, these threads highlight the multidimensional nature of human existence and the potential for spiritual growth beyond the physical realm.</u>

3. **The Exit of the Three Permanent Atoms:**

   The three permanent atoms, located in the solar plexus, pineal gland, and heart centre, serve as recording devices for emotional, mental, and spiritual experiences, respectively.

   Astral Seed Atom: Found in the solar plexus, it stores emotional imprints and experiences, contributing to the individual's journey beyond the physical realm. Associated with the astral body, it corresponds to emotions, desires, and the subconscious mind.

   Mental Seed Atom: Residing in the pineal gland, it records mental experiences, thoughts, beliefs, and intellectual patterns, facilitating transition to higher dimensions or states of consciousness. Associated with the mental body, it represents logic, intuition, and spiritual insight.

   Heart Seed Atom: Situated in the heart centre, it records experiences related to love, empathy, and spiritual connection, guiding the individual toward higher states of consciousness and union with the divine. Associated with the heart chakra, it governs emotional balance and unconditional love.

   Overall, these atoms play a vital role in the human energy system, recording and preserving individual experiences, emotions, thoughts, and connections across lifetimes and dimensions. They contribute to the karmic process of spiritual evolution and the transition between physical incarnations.

4. **The Exit of Etheric Astral and Mental Bodies:** The departure of the etheric, astral, and mental bodies from the physical body signifies the transition of consciousness to higher dimensions or states of existence, occurring at the time of death or during

certain spiritual experiences. Each of these bodies represents distinct aspects of consciousness and energy, facilitating the individual's journey beyond the physical plane. Here's a breakdown of each aspect:

Etheric Body: The subtle energy counterpart of the physical body, the etheric body serves as a blueprint for its structure and vitality. Its departure involves the dissolution of this energetic blueprint, allowing the individual's life force energy to transition beyond the physical form. This separation marks the beginning of exploration and evolution on spiritual planes.

Astral Body: Serving as the vehicle for emotions, desires, and subconscious impressions, the astral body exists on the multiple dimensions of the astral plane. Associated with experiences beyond the physical realm, such as dreams and out-of-body experiences, its detachment from the physical body enables exploration of other dimensions of consciousness. This transition opens pathways to heightened awareness, expanded consciousness, and spiritual growth.

Mental Body: The mental body serves as the conduit for thoughts, beliefs, and cognitive processes, operating on the mental plane of existence. Associated with reasoning, intuition, and spiritual insight, its departure entails the release of individual mental constructs and cognitive patterns from the physical brain. This transition enables deeper exploration of higher states of consciousness, spiritual truths, and universal wisdom beyond the limitations of the physical mind.

In summary, the exit of the etheric, astral, and mental bodies signifies the liberation of consciousness from the physical realm and the journey towards higher dimensions of existence. It represents the dissolution of energetic attachments and the expansion of awareness beyond the confines of the physical body, paving the way for spiritual evolution, enlightenment, and union with the divine.

5. **The Raising of the Kundalini and the Exit of the Personality.** The raising of the kundalini and the exit of the personality are intricately linked to the chakra through which the soul departs. Ideally, departure occurs through the crown chakra or the third eye, reflecting a focus on spiritual insight or divine connection.

   However, if the individual's focus in life was primarily astral, love-centred, or will-driven, the soul exits through corresponding chakras such as the solar plexus, heart, or throat. This chakra of departure influences the bardo experience, with every life event serving as preparation for this pivotal moment. Departure through the crown chakra is considered ideal.

HOW YOU CAN HELP SOMEONE TRANSITION

Alice Bailey in her book, *'Death: the Great Adventure'* highlights that the death experience should be supported by quietness, reverence, and peace. Hopefully all affairs of estate are in order to ease the mind of material concerns; and there is a legal statement requesting not to keep the person alive by mechanical means.

1. When death is nigh, burning an orange light in the room assists the upward flow of the kundalini to depart.
2. As the soul is in the process of deserting its habitation, it is essential that only sandalwood incense is burned. Sandalwood has the effect of breaking down old energies; which is needed at the time of death.

3. Quietly reminding the person to merge with the Clear Light of God and not to focus on anything else as they die is a beautiful support; along with the guidance to leave through the crown chakra.
4. Cross the feet and hands and if necessary, facilitate a last confession either with a friend, family member, or priest.
5. It is recommended to face the dying person eastward just as when meditating as the spiritual current is strongest when facing in this direction. However, different traditions and cultures may have their own preferred directions or orientations. Follow what resonates.
6. Pray to God and the master's for help in the process.
7. The Death Hormone has the capacity to allow the dying person to not feel any pain, so in the stages when death is evident, there is no need for drugs and the dying person can have some presence.
8. Soon after the death hormone is released shortly before death, a psychic tremor occurs. This assists in the release of the etheric connection which then disperses and dies.
9. In a highly spiritual person, this process can occur very rapidly. It is a slower process in a less evolved soul.
10. After the astral, mental, and spiritual bodies exit, the soul will find itself in a body that is appropriate for its level of spiritual evolution.

Now I lay me down to sleep, I pray the Lord my soul to keep
If I should die before I wake, I pray the Lord my soul to take.

AFTERWORD

**Operating from your God-self or Grace Over Drama
Can Bust your Karma**

Living in a state of enlightenment centres on embracing the loftiest virtues of humanity. When the unconscious fear matrix is dissolved, it allows you to return to a state of balance and supports the holistic well-being encompassing the physical, mental, and spiritual realms.

Moreover, enlightenment liberates you from the cycles of rebirth. An additional benefit is the dissolution of the astral body's negative emotions from the energy system, cutting off communion with the collective negative consciousness of the astral plane.

The Eye of the Storm

In today's chaotic world, the eye of the storm stands as a remarkable anomaly—a serene sanctuary amidst tempestuous upheaval. It is a realm of temporary peace and tranquillity, contrasting starkly with the turbulent forces that rage all around.

When you practice your deep colourful love-breathing with compassion, and authenticity the cacophony of chaos subsides. It is replaced by a peaceful calmness that permeates the atmosphere. The deafening roar of conflicts and uncertainties retreats, allowing moments of respite from the relentless pandemonium.

Within this stillness, your mind finds solace in temporary refuge. It is as if your personal world takes a collective breath, pausing to assess the magnitude of the whirlwind that surrounds it. The eye of the storm becomes a canvas for introspection, offering fleeting but powerful opportunities for clarity and insight.

Nature's laws, however, dictate that the eye's respite is short-lived. As quickly as you may find yourself engulfed in its tranquillity, the raging chaos beckons once more. The swirling forces converge upon the tranquil centre, pulling it back into the chaotic dance of existence.

This of course, gives you many perfect opportunities to maintain the practice of standing in your own magnificent power to recognise the Law of Rhythm and use the Law of Polarity to gain neutrality and further momentum.

The eye of the storm is a metaphor for the human spirit's resilience, a reminder that amidst the turmoil, there exists a capacity for composure and inner strength. It embodies your human instinct to seek refuge, to find a sense of equilibrium in the face of adversity.

In a chaotic world, finding the eye of the storm is a skill to be mastered – a moment to ground yourself amidst the chaos, to gather strength, and to emerge wiser, ready to confront the whirlwind once more.

It is a sanctuary of hope, reminding you that even amid the darkest turmoil, there remains a glimmer of serenity, a chance to restore balance, and the potential for renewal.

The eye of the storm is not a permanent shelter. To navigate a chaotic world, you must learn to adapt, to dance with the tempest, and to face the tumult head-on. It is through this interplay of calm and chaos that you evolve, grow, and discover the resilience of your human spirit.

You give yourself a chance to find the gift in every challenge. It is precisely in the eye of the storm that you find the strength to endure and the courage to forge a path towards a brighter and more harmonious future.

SIMPLICITY

In life's journey, I've learned that life's deepest lessons aren't found in scientific equations. Instead, they reside in the simple moments of stillness, self-reflection, and connection. It's about living a life that prioritises:

Harmlessness: Embracing harmlessness in your actions and words fosters a compassionate and peaceful environment, creating a positive ripple effect in your relationships and the world around you.

Presence: The most profound wisdom often comes from being fully present in the moment, whether it's savouring the taste of food, listening deeply to a friend, or witnessing the beauty of nature. Being present allows you to discover the richness of life.

Balance: Health isn't just the absence of illness; it's a harmonious balance of mind, body, and spirit. Nurturing your physical well-being, cultivating mental clarity, and tending to your emotional and spiritual growth are all essential components of a holistic, healthy life.

Compassion: The heart of wisdom lies in compassion. When you approach yourself and others with kindness and understanding, you create connections that heal, uplift, and transform. Compassion is a powerful force for personal and societal change.

Simplicity: Sometimes, the most profound truths are the simplest. By simplifying your life – reducing clutter, noise, and unnecessary complexity – you create space for clarity, joy, and a deeper connection with your true self.

Inner Knowing: There's a wisdom within each of us that goes beyond scientific explanations. It's the intuitive sense that guides your choices, the inner knowing that recognises what feels right and true. Trusting this inner wisdom can lead to a life of authenticity and fulfillment.

Connection: We're interconnected with all of life. Nurturing your relationships, fostering a sense of community, and recognising our shared humanity can bring a sense of purpose, belonging, and shared wisdom.

This philosophy isn't about rejecting science; it's about acknowledging that there are dimensions of our existence that science can't fully capture. It's about embracing the beauty of the unmeasurable, the power of the intangible, and the richness of your lived experiences.

It's a reminder that, in your pursuit of knowledge, you mustn't lose sight of the wisdom that resides in the simplicity of Being.

AFTERWORD

Thank you for reading this book
And taking a look
At the invisible world of your Being.
With the smut that is washed from your physical eyes
Your future is worthy of seeing.
For the thoughts you have and the love that you share
Are the keys to your Superior Being!

You'll understand that giving a hand
To your neighbour and enemy too.
And accepting yourself for all that you are
Will free the Spirit of YOU.

Always with love and blessings!
I AM that I AM
Pamm

A PRAYER FOR THE NEW AGE

"I am the creator of the Universe.
I am the Father and Mother of the Universe.
Everything came from Me.
Everything shall return to Me.
Mind, spirit, and body are My temples,
For the Self to realise in them
My Supreme Being and Becoming."
(Maitreya the Christ)

ABOUT THE AUTHOR

Introducing the 'I AM' that is Pamm Millage. With a mind that weaves tapestries of imagination and metaphor, Pamm has established herself as a creative force to be reckoned with, more especially within the fields of energy healing, the dynamics of ascension and soul psychology.

Pamm was introduced to spiritual psychotherapy and energy healing in the early seventies; although she had already noticed the effects of negative energy on herself and people around her when she was a child but did not have the knowledge or wisdom to rationalise it.

She has integrated a symphony of modalities into her hypnotherapy practice for the past three decades; bringing insight and compassion to her work and leaving a positive impact on the hearts of readers, colleagues, and clients across the globe.

Pamm is a Foundation Member and past President of the *New Zealand Association of Professional Hypnotherapists Inc (NZAPH)* – New Zealand's only not-for-profit association setting standards and ethics for Hypnotherapists in New Zealand and allied to the *Australian Hypnotherapy Association (AHA)*. Recently she was humbled to receive a lifetime honorary membership of the NZAPH for her dedicated services to hypnotherapy in New Zealand. She is a member of the *National Guild of Hypnotists* (NGH) in the US and a Reg. Prof. Member of *Hypnosis NZ* (HNZ).

Born in Devonport on the North Shore of Auckland, New Zealand, and nurtured by a childhood immersed in literature, Pamm developed an insatiable appetite for reading and storytelling from an early age, crafting a vibrant mosaic of inspiration for her onward journey. Drawing from literary masterworks in the exploration and intricacies of human and spiritual design, she adeptly infuses her unique voice to craft a literary style that is both timeless and distinctly her own.

Pamm readily acknowledges that within the eternal expanse of existence, nothing is entirely new. The essence lies in the manner of expression, determining whether it resonates with the hearts and minds of those who encounter her words.

Pamm's journey as a writer and healer has been one of dedication, service, and relentless pursuit of excellence. Her early works, often scribbled in the margins of notebooks, and re-discovered decades after their first writing, laid the foundation for her literary ambitions.

As she hones her craft, her writing begins to shine, illuminating the depths of human emotions and exploring the intricacies of the invisible aspects of human experience with astonishing clarity.

ABOUT THE AUTHOR

ASTRAL marks Pamm's inaugural full-length book, shifting her focus from previous endeavours encompassing short stories and e-books, newspaper and magazine articles, self-development guides, and therapeutic workshops.

In more recent manuscripts, Pamm fearlessly pushes the boundaries of limited belief, at times blurring the lines between what appears real and what seems fantasy. Her writings also materialise from her own personal experience to more vividly etch a deep and glorious reminder of parallels that already exist in the minds of her readers. All this while traversing landscapes both familiar and extraordinary.

Through her lyrical prose and meticulous attention to detail, Pamm invites readers to embark on transformative journeys that resonate long after the final page has been turned, which is the real purpose behind her writings.

Pamm expresses, *"It is uncanny that the clients who seek help in my clinic are often 90% primed and ready for healing, as if they have been directed my way. All that is necessary is a little guidance and Divine intervention when they are willing."*

She adds, *"I find joy in assisting people to experience the profound power of their own mind at its zenith, where they can rediscover the love and strength within. However, it's essential to remember that transformation can only occur when you are ready and willing to dedicate yourself to the process. No one else can do the work for you; it requires your active participation and commitment."*

Pamm can be contacted via email at: *pamm@pamm.nz*

ASTRAL

*"When you see and hear Me you will realise that you have known for long the Truths which I utter...These simple Truths, my friends, underlie all existence.
Sharing and Justice, Brotherhood and
Freedom are not new concepts.
From the dawn of time mankind has linked his aspiration to these beckoning stars. Now, my friends, shall we anchor them in the world."*
(Maitreya, the World Teacher)

GLOSSARY OF TERMINOLOGY

Lingo	Description
Astral Travel	The process of leaving the physical body and travelling in your emotional body to the astral plane.
Bardo	Self- Judgement Day or Bardo experience.
Delusion	A dangerously deceptive idea.
Discernment	Guiding yourself by spiritual observation done with impersonal love.
Divine	Spiritual or Holy.
Ego	A sense of self and individuality.
GOD	The Living Light creative source of ALL defined for humanity as 'man minus ego.' The Sacred Trinity of Love, Wisdom, Power.
God-self	The highest spiritual thought presence you can achieve on Earth, such as expressed by Christ, Buddha, Krishna, Moses, Sai Baba...

I AM that I AM	The English translation of the Hebrew name of God as revealed to Moses.
Illusion	Misperception resulting from a trick of the senses, or something that is not as it appears.
Karma	The Law of Cause and Effect – Also cycle of reincarnation.
Mass Consciousness	Combined thought, emotions, energy, and vibration of all souls currently in a low state of consciousness.
Negative Ego	Illusion that we are physical rather than spiritual beings.
Physical Being	Vehicle for soul to evolve and express itself.
Purpose	Specific reason for human being. Transcending negative ego and replacing with God-self in your service work on Earth.
Sin	Mistakes not indelible blemishes. Can be forgiven.
Soul	Intermediary between personality and Spirit or God-self.
Soul Travel	The process of leaving the physical body and traveling in your soul body on the inner spiritual planes.
Source	A term to describe God, or that which is the source of all love, light, and creative energy – the ALL.
Spirit	Another name for God (grounding Heaven to Earth).

BIBLIOGRAPHY

** Biophotons
- Champagne, CSK Mishra, Pascale (2009-01-01). IK International Pvt Ltd pp.363—ISBN 9789380026299. Retrieved 16 August 2012
- Rattemeyer M, Popp FA, Nagl, W (1981) Evidence of photon emission from DNA in living systems, Nature Wissenshanften, 68(11):672-573
- Popp, FA, Li, K, Giu.Q.(1992) Recent advances in biophoton research and its application, World scientific, 1-18.
- Popp, FA, Quao, G, KeOHsuen, L (1994) Biophoton emission: experimental background ad theoretical approaches, Modern Physics Letters B,8(21-22)
- Popp, FA, Chang JJ, Hersong, A, Yan, S, Yan, Y. (2002) Evidence of non-classical (squeezed) light in biological systems. Physics Letters A, 293(1-2): 98-102
- Cohen, S, Popp, FA (1997), Biophoton emission of the human body. Journal of Photochemistry and Photobiology B: Biology 40(2): 187-189

RECOMMENDED READING

There are too many spiritual and metaphysical books relevant to our discussion to name them all. Here are a few classics which relate.

Cartwright, Alexis 'Beyond Doorways' 4th Edition 2014

'Death: The Great Adventure' – Compilation by two students of Bailey, Alice A., and Te Tibetan Master, Djwhal Khul – Lucis Publishing 1985

'The Seven rays of Life' – Compilation by student of Alice A Bailey and The Tibetan Master, Djwhal Khul – Lucis Publishing 1995

Allen, James, "As a Man Thinketh" L N Fowler & Co, London. 1908

Allen, James, "Books of Meditation and Thoughts' 1909

Bailey, Alice A., 'Esoteric Psychology' Lucis Publishing Company 1942

Bailey, Alice A., 'The Rays and the Initiations' Lucis Publishing Company 1960

Bardon, Franz 'Initiation into Hermetics' Merkur Publishing 2007

Crème, Benjamin, 'The Ageless Wisdom' Share International 1996

Gawain, Shakti, "Creative Visualisation' Whatever Pub. 1948

Haanel, Charles F. 'The Master Key System' 1912

Hawkins, D.R. MD PhD, 'Power vs Force' Veritas Publishing 1995

Herbstreith, A., 'The Book of Life,' 1971

Herbstreith, A., 'The Laws of the Light – Hidden Secrets Revealed by IAM that IAM' 1971

Hurtak, J.J., 'The Book of Knowledge: The Keys of Enoch' Academy for Future Science, 1973

Lipton, B.H. PhD, 'The Biology of Belief' Hay House 2005

Louise L Hay, 'Heal Your Body' Specialist Publications – 1976

Martel, J, Les Editions 'The Complete Dictionary of Ailments and Diseases' Internationales 2011

Rachele, S., 'The Secrets of Unlimited Energy', 2020

Schucman, H., & Thetford, W., 'A Course in Miracles,' Foundation for Inner Peace, 1975

Stone, J.D. PhD., 'Ascension Activation Meditations of the Spiritual Hierarchy' Writers Club Press 2001

Stone, J.D. PhD., 'Beyond Ascension' Light Technology Publishing 1995

Stone, J.D. PhD., 'Golden Keys to Ascension and Healing' Light Technology Publishing 1998

Stone, J.D. PhD., 'Hidden Mysteries' Light Technology Publishing 1995

Stone, J.D. PhD., 'How to Teach Ascension Classes' Light Technology Publishing 1998

Stone, J.D. PhD., 'Manual for Planetary Leadership' Light Technology Publishing 1998

Stone, J.D. PhD., 'Soul Psychology' Random House 1994

Stone, J.D. PhD., 'The Ascended Masters Light the Way' Light Technology Publishing 1995

Stone, J.D. PhD., 'The Complete Ascension Manual' Light Technology Publishing 1994

Stone, J.D. PhD., 'The Golden Book of Melchizedek' Writers Club Press 2001

Stone, J.D. PhD., 'The Official IAM University and Company of Heaven Master Thesis on How to Become a Master Spiritual, Psychological, and Earthly Counsellor for Self and Others!' Vols I&II 2006

Stone, J.D. PhD., All volumes of 'The Encyclopaedia of the Spiritual Path '

Stone, Robert B. PhD, "Life Without Limits' Llewellyn Publishing 1988

Three Initiates, 'The Kybalion' Chicago, Ill., The Yogi publication society 1908 (Internet archives)

Tyson, D, Astral Projection & The Magical Universe, Llewellyn Publications 2007

Virtue, Doreen, PhD, 'Divine Magic' Hay House 2006

Weissmann, Darren R., 'The Power of Infinite Love and Gratitude' Hay House 2005

HANDY LINKS

Note: The reading of this book is a pre-requisite for registered professional hypnotherapists to take Pamm's signature course –
"The Infusion Protocol."

Please email pamm@pamm.nz directly for more information.

THE LAWS OF THE LIGHT BOOK
*Email **pamm@pamm.nz** for a free digital pdf*
NB: Type 'LIGHT' in the subject line to prevent delays.

Visit *https://www.pamm.nz* for a link to *HeartMath* Technology.

As a Certified *HeartMath* Practitioner, I have been successfully using *HeartMath* technology to aid patients and clients in using Harmonic Resonance Exercises in my practice since 2014. I can highly recommend this technology as a support for holistic health.

Visit *https://www.totalenlightenmentstore.com/*

This link will take you to the *I AM University* website where you will find courses, books, beautiful, guided meditations, and any number of supportive resources, including the study of spiritual psychology, to assist in integrating spirituality into your life.

If you prefer to read books, as I do, I can recommend any books written by the Founder of I AM University, the late Dr Joshua David Stone, PhD; some of which I have listed above.

LIGHT AND COLOUR TECHNOLOGY FOR PHYSICAL AND EMOTIONAL WELLBEING
Visit *https://bioptron.co.nz/*
Use 'Z354' as Agent Code in shop for free shipping

CLEAN AIR AND CLEAN WATER TECHNOLOGY
Visit *https://www.zepternz.co.nz*
Use 'Z354' as Agent Code

FIND A REGISTERED PROFESSIONAL HYPNOTHERAPIST IN NEW ZEALAND
https://www.nzaph.com/find-a-hypnotherapist
https://hypnosisnewzealand.co.nz/registeredhypnotherapists.html

FIND REGISTERED PROFESSIONAL HYPNOTHERAPISTS IN AUSTRALIA
https://www.ahahypnotherapy.org.au/find-a-hypnotherapist
https://www.pellenandpalmer.com/findahypnotherapist

FIND REGISTERED PROFESSIONAL HYPNOTHERAPISTS IN THE U.S.
https://ngh.net/find-hypnotists/

FIND AN EXCELLENT MENTORING PROGRAMME FOR HYPNOTHERAPISTS
https://bit.ly/32bUFNy
Use this DISCOUNT COUPON 'save200Pamm'

NOTES

ASTRAL

NOTES

ASTRAL

NOTES

ASTRAL

NOTES

www.ingramcontent.com/pod-product-compliance
Lightning Source LLC
Chambersburg PA
CBHW020135130526
44590CB00039B/185